Enter the Ancient World of the Norse

Norse Magic. These words conjure up shining images of adventurous Viking warriors, huge swords in hand, sailing their fabled dragon-ships over the foaming ocean. Like other ancient tribes, the Northmen had a strong bond to the Earth and the Elements, the Gods and the "little people."

In its practical, easy-to-understand format, *Norse Magic* offers important features that distinguish it from other books written about the Norse:

- In-depth discussion of the Norse pantheon, the Norse way of life and worship.
- Complete listings of Norse myths and deities
- Step-by-step instructions (including required tools and materials) for the immediate performance of spellwork and the practical application of magic in everyday life

"In the pages of *Norse Magic*, D.J. Conway gives the reader ready access and entry into the craft and ways of working with a kind of magic of the ancient North which runs parallel to that of the runes. She also gives us insight into the art and practice of *seith*—the magical way of the Lady, Freyja."

Edred Thorsson
Yrmin-Drighten of the Rune-Gild
Author of *Rune Might*
A Book of Troth

About the Author
D.J. Conway was born in Hood River, Oregon to a family of Irish-North Germanic-American Indian descent. She began her quest for knowledge of the occult more than twenty-five years ago, and has been involved in many aspects of New Age religion from the teachings of Yogananda to study of the Qabala, healing, herbs, ancient pantheons and Wicca. Although an ordained minister in two New Age churches and holder of a Doctor of Divinity degree, Conway claims that her heart lies within the pagan cultures. No longer actively lecturing and teaching as she did for years, Conway has centered her energies on writing.

To Write to the Author
If you wish to contact the author or would like more information about this book, please write to the author in care of Llewellyn Worldwide, and we will forward your request. Both the author and publisher appreciate hearing from you and learning of your enjoyment of this book and how it has helped you. Llewellyn Worldwide cannot guarantee that every letter written to the author can be answered, but all will be forwarded. Please write to:

D.J. Conway
c/o Llewellyn Worldwide
P.O. Box 64383, Dept. L137-7, St. Paul, MN 55164-0383, U.S.A.
Please enclose a self-addressed, stamped envelope for reply, or $1.00 to cover costs.
If outside the U.S.A., enclose international postal reply coupon.

Llewellyn's World Magic Series

Norse Magic

D.J. Conway

2003
Llewellyn Publications
St. Paul, Minnesota 55164-0383, U.S.A.

FIRST EDITION
Seventh printing, 2003

Cover art by Lissanne Lake

Library of Congress Cataloging-in-Publication Data
Conway, D.J. (Deanna J.)
    Norse magic / by D.J. Conway.
        p.   cm. — (Llewellyn's world magic series)
    Includes bibliographical references.
    ISBN 0-87542-137-7
    1. Magic, Norse. 2. Mythology, Norse.
    I. Title. II. Series.
BF1622.N66C65 1990
133.4'3'089395—dc20

                                                            90-6204
                                                            CIP

Llewellyn Publications
A Division of Llewellyn Worldwide, Ltd.
P.O. 64383, St. Paul, MN 55164-0383
www.llewellyn.com

Printed in the United States of America

LLEWELLYN'S WORLD MAGIC SERIES

At the core of every religion, at the foundation of every culture, there is MAGIC.

Magic sees the World as *alive*, as the home which humanity shares with beings and powers both visible and invisible with whom and which we can *interface* to either our advantage or disadvantage—depending upon our awareness and intention.

Religious worship and communion is one kind of magic, and just as there are many religions in the world so are there many magical systems.

Religion, and magic, are ways of seeing and relating to the *creative* powers, the *living* energies, the *all-pervading* spirit, the *under-lying* intelligence that is the universe within which we and all else exist.

Neither Religion nor Magic conflict with Science. All share the same goals and the same limitations: always seeking Truth, forever haunted by human limitations in perceiving that truth. Magic is "technology" based upon experience and *extra-sensory insight*, providing its practitioners with methods of greater influence and control over the world of the invisible before it impinges on the world of the visible.

The study of world magic not only enhances your understanding of the world in which you live, and hence your ability to *live better*, but brings you into touch with the *inner essence* of your long evolutionary heritage and most particularly—as in the case of the magical system identified most closely with your genetic inheritance—with *the archetypal images and forces most alive in your whole consciousness*.

Other Books by D.J. Conway

Celtic Magic
Maiden, Mother, Crone
Dancing With Dragons
By Oak, Ash & Thorn
Animal Magick
Flying Without a Broom
Moon Magick
Falcon Feather & Valkyrie Sword
The Dream Warrior (fiction)
Magical, Mythical, Mystical Beasts
Lord of Light and Shadow
Magick of the Gods & Goddesses
Soothslayer (fiction)
Shapeshifter Tarot (with Sirona Knight)
Perfect Love
The Mysterious, Magickal Cat
Warrior of Shadows (fiction)
Celtic Dragon Tarot (with Lisa Hunt)

CONTENTS

Elf Magic
Dwarf Magic
Rune Magic

1. Norse Magic and Its Uses Today

The Norse—adventurous Viking wanderers, daring warriors, worshippers of the Aesir and the Vanir (the Asa-Gods)—these words conjure up shining images of helmet-clad men, huge swords in hand, sailing their dragon-ships over the foaming ocean. People think of them as Scandinavians, and they were; but they also settled parts of northern Germany, northern France, and throughout the British Isles, leaving much of their culture, beliefs, and racial blood in these areas.

Like Celtic tribes, the Northmen had strong ties with the Earth and the Elements, the Gods, and the "little people" or "hidden people." From them come many of our ideas about trolls, dwarves, elves and giants. They believed in an afterlife and the end of the world, or Ragnarök, long before Christians ever infiltrated their culture. They gave us the concept of the Thing, or Assembly, where justice was administered. Theirs was one of the few cultures where women had a great amount of freedom and protection under the law.

Everywhere they went, the Northmen left their cultural influence. They ranged to the north and west as far as the shores of North America, Iceland and Greenland. To the south, they reached the balmy climate of the Mediterranean. The cultural acquisition was not one-sided. When they returned to their northern villages, these Vikings brought with them new ideas, fashions and fads from the countries they visited. These new ideas did not cause a breakdown in the Viking culture, as they did in many other cultures, because the Northmen applied them in such a way as to strengthen their position as wolf-warriors and shrewd traders of the northern seas.

Norse women were among the most liberated of the time. They had a considerable amount of freedom and status. The Norse concept of marriage allowed great cooperation and companionship between husband and wife. In addition to housewives, there were priestesses, wise women, rune-mistresses, healers and warriors.They could go before the Assembly and be granted justice, or even a divorce, just as the men could. Women were listened to by their men, especially if they had prophetic dreams or impressions. Dreams were considered important, as they were one of the ways that the gods contacted humans.

The people of this northern culture were individualists and deeply resented any attempt to curb their freedom. At the same time they were capable of great self-control, accepting adversities without self-pity. Any man prepared to die for what he believed was important was held in high esteem by friend and foe alike.

Many of their leaders were men of culture, discrimination, and wit. The Northmen loved a good story and a jest. They were shrewd traders with a wily instinct for commerce. They appreciated fine design and artistry, treasuring their ships and swords as much for their beauty as their utility. In the Viking culture, a quick-witted poet could win fame and fortune just as well as a brilliant swordsman. Anyone who was both had the world at his or her feet.

The Northmen were firm believers in retaliation for injustices. There was no room for softness or the doormat theory of existence. Their land was harsh and their lives fraught with hardship. Nevertheless, they maintained a strong belief in family and clan; stories and legends show immense, tender love for spouse, children, friends and family.

Their deities were strong, but not immortal. These gods and goddesses were pictured as men and women, only on a grander scale; wiser, stronger, more beautiful, guardians of humankind. The Vikings could understand and easily relate to this type of divine being.

Celtic magic and Norse magic are the only two true Western European magical traditions. They reflect the peoples who believed in them. The Northmen were among the last European societies to fall to Christianity.

Norse magic for today fits the type of personality that is a "doer," someone who definitely does not believe in taking a servile approach to life. It interests those who advocate actively shaping their own future, those who affirm that practicing spellwork is preferable to passively waiting for changes to come.

Norse magic enlists the help of the Asa-Gods, the Light Elves and good Dwarves. It elicits aid from dead ancestors and the rulers of the Elements. It is an active magic, reserved for participants, not by-standers. It is a magic of pride in oneself, courage to face whatever comes and continuing knowledge to mold the results to fit a particular life plan. Only a strong person, open to changes and the acceptance of new ideas, one willing to study and learn and put into practice the new knowledge, can hope to benefit from the practice of Norse magic. The Asa-Gods do not drop results into your lap. These gods only help those who help themselves.

You must attune yourself to the powers of the Elements, calling upon the Asa-Gods and other supernatural beings, and disregarding the old cry "Magic doesn't work!"

Magic works if you think it works. Preparing for magic begins with the subconscious mind, reprogramming it to accept the unseen, the disprovable. It begins with learning how to unlock the door to the creative part of the mind, or the right brain. True magic is the way of the individual, not society. It manifests itself in self-growth, improvement of life conditions, a restructuring of thought and living. If you can become successful and happy through magic, why worry about the opinions of others who are less open? Learn, practice, perform. Reap the benefits of Norse magic, and enjoy every new success to the fullest.

As the Old Norse would say: May the Gods of Asgard guide your steps. May Thorr's hammer protect you. May Freyja give you wisdom and magical power, and may Freyr grant you prosperity.

2. Understanding Norse Magic

What is ritual magic? Everyone has a mental picture of a ceremonial magician gesturing with his wand, a witch stirring her cauldron, or something similar. But that is not magic; that is only the physical activity that helps to perform ritual magic. These gestures and physical practices are necessary, but they are not the power. Nor are they the definition of the power.

Some have called magic "the art of changing consciousness at will." My own definition is less grand a statement. Ritual magic is the taking of energy from another plane of existence and weaving that energy by specific thoughts, words, and practices into a desired physical form or result.

Magic opens the door to the secret chamber of your mind, the chamber that contains infinite power to change you, your personal circumstances and your future. This secret chamber is a combination of the right brain, or the creative hemisphere, and the subconscious mind.

The human brain is divided into the left and

right hemispheres. The left brain generally maintains control; it likes and demands logic, order, routine, explicit functions and directions. It is the dominant side. It is also the side that criticizes us for things we do or do not do. It is closely connected with the conscious mind. The left brain deals totally with what it calls reality.

The right brain is the creative side, the artistic hemisphere. It likes creative activity in all its forms. It has unlimited powers to accomplish things that are important to it. It also is connected with the subconscious mind. The right brain deals entirely with what we call imagination.

In order to bring about permanent changes, the subconscious mind must be reprogrammed. Our subconscious minds are programmed from before birth, and most strongly from the day we are born. Every time we are told as children "You can't do that," "You shouldn't do that," "I love you when you do that," and the words are followed by an action that shows displeasure or approval, the subconscious mind permanently records the message: "It doesn't pay to do that," or "That got me noticed." The same applies when people laugh or make fun of you when you try to do something.

This type of programming continues throughout your life. That is why it is so important to choose friends carefully. Of course, we must have some rules to prevent us doing harm to ourselves and others. But it does seem such a shame to spend valuable adult years undoing "good intentions" or shifted problems that rightfully belonged to your friends, parents and teachers. However, this reprogramming must be done so you can experience your rightful complete potential.

Unfortunately, although most friends, parents, teachers, and society in general are well-meaning in their intentions, we are almost constantly being programmed for limitations and failures. One of the biggest stumbling blocks to effective magic are these deeply buried false limitations that tell us "You can't do that." Removing these restraints that make us doubt our abilities is like removing shackles.

Both the right brain and the subconscious mind perform best when presented with symbols. They do not react much, if at all, to verbal commands or desires, unless those commands are reinforced by a physical action that brings pain or pleasure. Thus, in working magic, all the spells, candles, tools, chants, etc. become symbols which the secret mind chamber, or right brain, readily accepts and uses to create the desired effect.

But, you may say, the left brain will interfere; it is not disposed to creativity. True. However, the very act of magical gesturing, reciting spells, laying out Tarot cards and all the other physical parts of magic deceives our analytical, do-something-worthwhile, left brain. It becomes so involved in taking an active, physical, logical part in the ritual, that it forgets to monitor and control the creative activity of the right brain.

The more emotionally involved you are in spellwork, the more creative activity happens in that secret chamber. The more creative activity there is, the stronger the message to the subconscious mind that we definitely desire a specific change to happen. The subconscious, reacting to input much like a computer, will implement the instructions.

When we speak of the use of emotions in magic, we mean controlled emotions, not a vacillating, rollercoaster-ride of emotions. Controlled emotional input in ritual proves to the subconscious mind that you are sincere in your desires and what you are attempting to accomplish.

Repetition plays a great part in this implementation. The ancients were wise in their insistence on the magical power numbers of 3, 5, 7 and 9. Doing spellwork for 3, 5, 7 or 9 days, consecutively, reinforces the creative activity in the secret chamber and underlines your message "I want this to happen!" Repetition becomes the pleasure-pain motivator that changes the programming of the subconscious mind.

To work magic effectively, you must believe you can cause things to happen, that you have the power within you to change your life. You must believe that it is within your power to take a desire, an emotional thought without physical substance, and manifest it in the material world. At first this may be difficult. Until you get your subconscious mind reprogrammed in a more positive manner, manifestations will take longer to appear.

Work on yourself: how you think of yourself, how you treat others (lying, cheating, stealing, broken promises, addictive habits). Keep practicing the spellwork. Quite unexpectedly, you will find everything coming together on a positive path. The magical results will flow from the secret mind chamber into your physical world, carrying with it health, happiness and prosperity.

I have heard too many times that you should not do magic for yourself, that it is selfish and wrong. This erroneous idea is a hold-over from Judeo-Christian belief, and has nothing whatsoever to do with magic. If you can't manifest through magic for yourself, you have little chance of manifesting for others. The Norse deities were and are greatly concerned about humankind, the Earth and all happenings within their vast realms. Therefore, how can we belittle anything that improves us or our surroundings?

This line of reasoning brings us to a rule of morality in magic: Do what you will if you harm no being. It will never be to your benefit to deliberately harm another being through magic. This includes taking away by magic something that belongs to another, such as a lover, spouse, job, etc. (I believe it is an exellent idea to put a copy of this rule in your ritual room.)

Let's look at this from the viewpoint of a lover. Suppose you are convinced you really want someone else's lover. Logically, there must be a very good karmic reason for those two people to be together.

If you use a spell to draw someone to you in that manner, not only will you have to live with whatever karmic problems they bring, but you will be building karmic debt of your own for controlling someone against his or her will. Believe me, you do not want to deal with any unnecessary karma; everyone has enough of their own to handle. Besides you could be passing up a greater and better love by narrowing your vision.

Also, if that person comes to you through spellworking, against his or her will, you will have to do a lifetime of magic to make certain he/she stays and does not leave you for someone else. What you fight to get through the misuse of magical power, you have to fight to keep.

When it comes to protecting yourself and your loved ones, the rule still holds. By no means be a door mat! But be creative in forming protective spellwork. Troublesome neighbors can be spelled to move. If they are engaged in illegal or destructive activities, justice can be brought down on them through the police and legal system. A harassing landlord can be influenced to treat you better, or you can spell for a better place to live.

It is essential to think through your reasons for doing magic. Brainstorm on paper, if necessary, until you are certain you are aware of all the options, have not limited yourself or destructively harmed others.

There is an old teaching called the Four Powers of the Magus (Magician): to know, to dare, to will, to be silent. Simply explained, it means to gain the knowledge needed to do ritual magic, to dare to practice it, to will the desired results, and to keep quiet about what you are doing. The last is especially important. Talking about spellwork dissipates the magical energy. Besides, many of your "friends" and family will torpedo your rituals by negative thoughts, intentionally or unintentionally, out of jealousy, spite, or fear of losing control over you. The practice of magic in this busy world is difficult enough without adding to the problem.

Moon phases play an important part in many

rituals. It is traditional that spellworking for decrease or removal of problems takes place from after the Full Moon until the New Moon, with the day or night of the New Moon being strongest. Spellworking for increase, growth and gain takes place from after the New Moon until the Full Moon, with the day or night of the Full Moon being the most powerful.

If you think about the effect of the Moon on the tides of the Earth, you will see the logical reasoning behind this. The greater part of the human body is made up of water or liquids. Therefore, like the waters of Earth, we are affected by the Moon and her phases. The type of energy from the phases of the Moon will be reflected in our bodies. It is better for spellworking to operate with the flow of energy than against it.

The last of this discussion on the definition of magic is a brief clarification of two types of ritual magic: evocation and invocation. Evocation is the commanding of certain forces and entities by Names of Power and sigils. These rituals are done in a mixture of Greek, Hebrew and unknown languages. They are ordinarily based on a framework of Judaism or Christianity. The compelled entity is forced into a magical triangle drawn outside the circle. Only the lower orders of spirits are evoked, and it can be extremely dangerous if you do not know exactly what you are doing.

Invocation is the safest and easiest form of magic to perform. It invites higher spirits and the gods to enter into the magical circle itself. This type of ritual does not use strange tongues and is never a command. It is much more harmless to invoke than evoke. This book will deal only with invocations.

3. Preparing for Magic

To begin the practice of magic, one must learn certain basic techniques: concentration, focusing, meditation, imaging. Along with actual doing, or practice, these techniques are essential to accomplishing physical manifestation by spellworking.

Concentration is holding an image or idea in your mind without interruption. Concentration is of prime importance during actual rituals when everything not directly related to what you are doing must be excluded from your thoughts. You must be so involved in your ritual and why you are doing it that no extraneous noise, no thoughts of the day's happenings, not even the telephone, is allowed to intrude into your mind. If they do intrude, they are immediately dismissed to be dealt with at another time.

There are two exercises that will strengthen your powers of concentration. Cut out a white dot about the size of a quarter and paste it against a dark background. Sit comfortably and look at the dot. Do not stare; blink your eyes whenever you need to do so. After a few minutes, close your eyes and look for the white dot. You will see it in front of you as if your eyes were still open. Keep your thoughts on that dot, and see how long you can maintain its image in your mind.

Another similar exercise uses a candle flame. Proceed in the same manner by looking at the flame. It is easiest on the eyes to look at the blue around the lower part of the wick instead of the bright upper flame. Close your eyes and concentrate on seeing the image, the same way you did with the white dot.

Focusing is adjusting your "inner eye" or attention on a particular object or goal. It is different from concentration, yet is an integral part of it. Focusing your "inner eye," or third eye, on a goal helps you to visualize the objective more clearly. Visualization, coupled with emotion and determination, is necessary to unlock the secret mind chamber, to start the process which fulfills your desires.

It really is not necessary to visualize the goal in complete detail; in fact, it is probably better not to decide on the last jot and tittle. Too much detail limits the manifestation, in that you could have had something better. It is rather like asking for a Ferrarri, but refusing to accept a blue one because you visualized only red.

Focusing and concentrating on what you are doing in ritual channels your mind's powers and energies into the activity, strengthening and clarifying it. For example, the act of casting a circle (which I will explain later) needs focusing and concentration to be done properly. If not done correctly, the circle will not adequately protect you or contain the magical energy you are raising.

Again, as exercises, we will use the candle flame and the white dot, but with a slightly different twist. This time as you concentrate on the white dot image in your mind, allow your creative right brain to summon up related ideas. The dot is white; it is round; it looks like the sun on a foggy day. Relax, and let these creative images pop through the door of your secret chamber. You may find that after a few minutes the dot changes color, or that you can make it change color. Summon up more images to fit the new color.

Go through the same exercise using the candle flame. See if you can make the flame go higher, expand, change color. Again, summon up all associated images.

In the practice of meditation, you use your powers of focusing, concentration, imaging, and relaxation to center yourself, control destructive emotions, and gain insight. Meditation also brings a heightened sense of awareness and increased ability to visualize. All of these skills are valuable in practicing magic and gaining practical results from magical rituals.

There is no reason that meditation need be a complicated procedure. Begin by selecting a piece of smooth, calm music that appeals to you. Classical music without singing or voices will provide a gentle background to screen out small noises and give your left brain something on which it can concentrate. Hang a "do not disturb" sign on your door, turn off the telephone, and sit comfortably in a chair.

Close your eyes and listen to the music while taking a few deep breaths. Mentally, surround yourself with white light. Imagine yourself standing beside an old fashioned well, the kind with a stone wall around it. One by one, drop all your problems into the well—relationships, finances, fears, everything. Then visualize yourself turning around, walking away. This technique is giving the left brain something to think about, while the symbology of the action is influencing the right brain to come up with an answer to solving those problems. The right brain only understands symbols, remember?

To continue the meditation, project yourself into a beautiful, peaceful garden. Wander along the paths; soak up the peacefulness, the healing, the calmness that exists in that garden. You may see people and buildings. Go where you like; talk with people; take part in ceremonies.

As long as you remain objective in your outlook, you can receive amazing guidance in this other-plane garden. However, once you push to hear what you want to hear, the clear messages will cease. You will get only feed-back from your left brain and conscious mind.

Anytime you wish to end the meditation, just become aware of your body and open your eyes. You will find that time has absolutely no meaning while in meditation. The same phenomenon occurs when you are involved in magical ritual. The limiting idea of time belongs only to the left brain and the conscious mind.

Perhaps you realized while reading the above

meditation that, while in that other-plane garden, you were exercising your concentration, focusing and imaging abilities. Meditation is a nice way to strengthen these while gaining the fringe benefits of relaxation, often healing on the physical, mental and emotional levels.

With a little practice, you can visualize going directly from the well to a temple or a class or a meeting with a specific person who talked with you during your meditations. Please remember to be courteous, as these personalities are not necessarily figments of your imagination. All existence does not belong exclusively to this physical level of life. Also practice discrimination, the same as you would when meeting any new acquaintance. From time to time it is possible to meet someone in your "travels" who will not be the kind of being you wish to be around. If one of these types appears, recall the white light and leave.

It is a wise precaution always to begin meditation by surrounding yourself mentally with the white light, followed by a stop at the well. This is a protection that eliminates carrying negative vibrations into the meditation, vibrations that could contaminate an otherwise beautiful productive experience.

4. Magical Elements

All magic is primarily based on four Elements for spellworking. These Elements are Air, Fire, Water and Earth. As we discuss these magical Elements, you will see that they influence our physical world more than we realize, as well as influencing our personalities and the realm of magic.

The four Elements correspond to the four directions of our physical world, the four quarters of the universe, and most importantly to the four quarters of the magic circle. They are forces and types of substance that make up the universe and everything in it. Science, with its limited knowledge, does not acknowledge these four Elements as building blocks in the same way that the magician does. But science does agree that they exist, although scientists call them by other names.

The four Elements possess form as well as force. Each has certain qualities, natures, moods, and purposes. Each can be called a kingdom; each has a ruler or king; each has positive and negative traits. Because the magician calls to each Element to protect its quarter of the circle and to render aid, it is important to understand exactly what each of these Elements is and does.

The Element of Air governs the eastern quarter of the circle. Its ruler is Paralda who oversees the Sylphs, Zephyrs, and nature spirits or fairies. Its color is pure yellow; it is considered warm and moist. The positive associations of Air are: sunrise, Spring, incense, the wand, clouds, breezes, breath, optimism, joy, intelligence, mental quickness, any kind of helpful air. Negative associations of Air are: frivolity, gossip, fickleness, inattention, bragging, forgetfulness, wind storms, tornadoes, hurricanes, destructive air in any form.

The Element of Fire governs the southern quarter of the circle. Its ruler is Djin (dee-yin) who oversees the Salamanders, Firedrakes, and the little ones of the sunbeams. Its color is pure red; it is considered warm and dry. The positive associations of Fire are: noon, Summer, the dagger and sword, candles, any kind of helpful fire, the Sun, stars, blood, enthusiasm, activity, courage, daring, willpower, leadership. Negative associations of Fire are: hate, jealousy, fear, anger, war, ego, conflicts, lightning, volcanoes, harmful fire of any kind.

The Element of Water governs the western quarter of the circle. Its ruler is Niksa who oversees the Nymphs, Undines, Mer-people, and the little ones of springs, lakes, ponds, and rivers. Its color is pure blue; it is cold and moist. The positive associations of Water are: sunset, Fall, the chalice and cauldron, any form of helpful water, compassion, peacefulness, forgiveness, love, intuition. Negative associations of Water are: floods, rain storms, whirlpools, any kind of harmful water, laziness, indifference, instability, lack of emotional control, insecurity.

The Element of Earth (the Element most familiar to beings of this planet) governs the northern quarter. Its ruler is Ghob, sometimes called Ghom, who oversees the gnomes and dwarves, and the little ones of the moonbeams. Its color is clear dark green; it is cold and dry. The positive associations of Earth are: Winter, midnight, the pentacle, ritual salt, gemstones, mountains, caves, soil, respect, endurance, responsibility, stability, thoroughness, purpose in life. Negative associations of Earth are: rigidity, unwillingness to change, stubbornness, lack of conscience, vacillation, earthquakes, slides.

There is a fifth Element, Spirit, which dominates the center of the magical circle and balances all the other Elements. Through Spirit, or invocation of the Gods, we blend the various Elements needed to bring forth the manifestation of our desires.

The rulers of the Elements and their kingdoms are represented in their respective quarters by a symbol and perhaps a candle of the appropriate color. At the beginning of the ritual, and starting in the east, the magician welcomes the Element of Air. Moving clockwise around the circle he welcomes each Element, ending in the north. When the ritual is finished, the magician thanks and dismisses each Element, again beginning in the east and moving clockwise around the circle. Finally, before the magic circle is officially opened, the magician should return to the center and thank "all beings in the visible and invisible."

This is the dismissal for Spirit.

In Norse mythology, when the worlds were created Odhinn and his brothers set four Dwarves permanently in place to hold up the sky at the four directions. These Dwarves can be considered as ruling the four directions and Elements. They are Nordhri (North, ruling ice), Austri (East, ruling air), Sudhri (South, ruling fire), and Vestri (West, ruling water). The Norse considered the Earth in the center as balance. You may call upon these Dwarves as Rulers of the four Elements if you wish.

5. *Casting the Magic Circle*

The magic circle, cast by dagger or sword, is an imaginary boundary (to the physical eye), but when properly drawn, has great power both in this and other realms. The energy of the circle's boundary keeps out negative influences. It also serves to contain the power raised within the circle until the magician releases it. Its primary function is to create a safe, regenerating working area for the performance of magic.

The power raised within the magic circle is commonly called the Cone of Power. On the astral level, the shape of this Cone of Power, when properly produced, is a pulsating cone of energy, with its point high above the ritual area.

Some say that the circle must only have a nine-foot circumference. However, I have cast circles just big enough to stand in and others that took in a fifteen-foot room. All were powerful because of the concentration and visualization used when they were cast.

All needed supplies for spellworking, including the Element candles, must be inside the ritual area before the circle is drawn. Once cast and sealed, it is wise never to cross the boundary until the ritual or spellworking is finished and the Elements dismissed. Cats, however, have the unusual ability of being able to cross the cast circle without disturbing the power flow. I have no explanation for this; I only know it is so.

The wand, in Wiccan rites, directs magical power and is used to persuade. The athame (dagger) or sword, being of steel or iron and having a sharp point, traditionally is used for defense and banishing.

Casting a proper circle requires concentrated visualization and focusing of inner energy on the part of the magician. To do this, hold the consecrated dagger or sword (see later chapter for consecration rituals) in your power or dominant hand. The dominant hand is generally considered the hand with which you write. Begin at the eastern quarter of the area to be circled. Aim the ritual tool at the floor or ground while visualizing an intense silver-blue light issuing from its tip. Using that light, "draw" a circle clockwise to cover your ritual area. Finish by overlapping the ends of the line in the east. The circle does not have to be perfectly round. What is important is that you see, at least with your inner eye, a boundary line of silver-blue flame around you.

The symbols and/or candles of each Element are now set just inside the boundary line. Welcome each Element in its proper quarter before concentrating on your spellworking. Remember to dismiss the Elements at the end of the proceedings before you open the circle.

When you are finished with your work, "cut" the circle with a backwards, or reverse, movement of your sword or dagger across a section of the boundary. The silver-blue circle will wink out of existence.

SAMPLE RITUAL

Gather everything you will need for your altar and spellworking. Place on or near your altar the following items: materials needed for any particular spellworking, a chalice with a little spring or fresh water in it; a dish of salt, pentacle disk (see chapter on Magical Tools) your sword and/or dagger, wand, incense burner (preferably one with attached chains for carrying) with lighted charcoal; incense, one or two altar candles for light, four Element candles. Once the magical circle is cast, you will not be crossing it until the ritual is finished.

A word here on incense and charcoal tablets. The best kind of incense is the kind burned on charcoal. Please use the little self-lighting charcoal tablets specially made for incense and NOT the barbecue ones!

Incense has an effect on the mind and emotions, appealing to the subconscious mind and past memories. This mental/emotional effect plus the atmosphere of a candle-lit room and the wearing of robes can transform any ritual area into a pagan shrine of magical power. You need to create this atmosphere in which magic can work.

Position your altar table in the center, facing north. The symbols and/or candles for the Elements should be set just inside the circle boundary with the altar set in the center. When you become more adept at spellworking, you can turn the central altar so that you face the predominant Element to be used in the spelling, if you wish.

Play soft instrumental music; it lends atmosphere. Relax, take a few deep breaths to center yourself.

Take your dagger or sword in your power hand. Starting in the east, visualize that powerful, protective silver-blue light shooting from the tip of your ritual tool. Aim it at the floor. Moving clockwise from the east, draw the magical boundary of the circle. Remember to overlap the ends in the east when you finish. While you are drawing the circle, say:

> *I consecrate this circle of power to the*
> *   Ancient Gods.*
> *Here may they manifest and bless their*
> *   child.*

Move back to the altar, facing north. Raise your dagger or wand in greeting, say:

> *This is a time that is not a time, in a*
> *   place that is not a place, on a day that*
> *   is not a day.*
> *I stand at the threshold between the*
> *   worlds before the Gates of Asgard.*
> *May the Ancient Ones help and protect*
> *   me on my magical journey.*

Set the water chalice on the pentacle disk. Hold your dagger over it and say:

> *Great Goddess Freyja, bless this*
> *creature of Water to your service.*
> *May we always remember the cauldron*
> *waters of rebirth.*

Hold your dagger over the salt, say:

> *Great Goddess Freyja, bless this*
> *creature of Earth to your service.*
> *May we always honor the blessed Earth,*
> *its many forms and beings.*

Sprinkle a little salt into the water, then hold the chalice up high. Say:

> *Great Freyja, be you adored!*

Beginning in the east and moving clockwise, sprinkle the water-salt mixture lightly around the edges of your circle. Replace the chalice on the altar. Hold your dagger over the lighted incense burner, saying:

> *Great God Freyr, bless this creature of*
> *Fire to your service.*
> *May we always remember the sacred*
> *Fire that dances within the form of*
> *every creation.*

Hold your dagger over the incense, saying:

> *Great God Freyr, bless this creature of*
> *Air to your service.*
> *May we always listen to the spirit*
> *winds that bring us the voices of the*
> *Ancient Ones.*

Put a little incense on the lighted charcoal in the burner. Don't put too much incense in the burner as a little goes a long way in an enclosed room! Using the attached chains, touch the burner briefly to the pentacle disk, then raise the burner high, saying:

Great Freyr, be you adored!

Carry the burner around the circle clockwise, beginning in the east. Return it to the altar.

Go to the eastern quarter of the circle and light the yellow candle. Hold up your hand in greeting. You may also salute the Element with your dagger, sword or wand instead of your hand:

I call upon you, Powers of Air, to witness this rite and to guard this circle.

Move to the south; light the red candle and hold up your hand in greeting:

I call upon you, Powers of Fire, to witness this rite and to guard this circle.

In the western quarter you light the blue candle and greet the Element:

I call upon you, Powers of Water, to witness this rite and to guard this circle.

End by going to the north; light the green candle and greet the Element:

I call upon you, Powers of Earth, to witness this rite and to guard this circle.

Move back to your central altar, and stand facing north. Raise your arms in greeting:

This circle is bound,
With power all around.
Within it I stand
With protection at hand.

Proceed with your planned spellwork or ceremony. When everything is completed, hold your hand or ritual tool over the altar and say:

By the powers of the ancient Gods,
I bind all power within this circle
Into this spell. So mote it be!

When you are ready to end the ritual, go to the east and extinguish the yellow candle. Say:

Depart in peace, O Powers of Air.
My thanks and blessings.

Go to the south and extinguish the red candle. Say:

Depart in peace, O Powers of Fire.
My thanks and blessings.

Go to the west and extinguish the blue candle. Say:

Depart in peace, O Powers of Water.
My thanks and blessings.

Finish by going to the north and extinguish the green candle. Say:

Depart in peace, O Powers of Earth.
My thanks and blessings.

Return to the center to stand before the altar.

Raise your arms and say:

> *To all beings and powers of the visible*
> *and invisible, depart in peace.*
> *May there always be harmony between*
> *us.*
> *My thanks and blessings.*

Cut the circle with a backwards motion of your magical tool to release all remaining vestiges of power for manifestation. Say:

> *The circle is open, yet ever it remains a*
> *circle.*
> *Around and through me always flows its*
> *magical power.*

Put away all magical tools and clear the altar, except for any candles or objects which must remain to either burn out or be empowered for a period of time specific for the ritual.

You have completed your ritual. Practice will make the power flow easier. Soon you will find that you look forward to ritual and spellworking.

6. Tools of Magic

To use Norse magic correctly, you must respond positively to active participation in magical rituals. You must be willing to do spellwork, to learn the self-discipline and emotional involvement required to get results.

One of the most important rules of magic is to do the work necessary for the results you want and KEEP SILENT about what you are doing. Silence gives your spellwork room to grow without being hindered or destroyed by negative thought-forms from others. The fewer people who know what you are doing, the better. The only time this rule does not apply is when you are working with like-minded people who are in complete agreement with your goals. Then the magical power is amplified.

Magic can be done with a minimum of tools: a working space or altar, dagger and cauldron. The full range of basic tools for Norse magic-work are: dagger or sword or both, goblets or drinking horns, cauldron, incense burner, wand, offering bowl and plate, candles with holders, runestones, various colored cords, special stones to entice Elves and

Dwarves. Optional implements are a small bell, horn and staff.

Music by Richard Wagner is a very appropriate aid also. Some of his music deals totally with the Norse-Germanic deities. Find recordings with instrumentals only; vocals can be too distracting. However, music you make for yourself can be a good active part of rituals.

The first magical tool you should get is an altar and a stone slab for its top. The altar itself may be a coffee table or chest that doubles as regular furniture. Or it may be a separate item that you use only for ritual work. If you are fortunate enough to have, or purchase, such furniture with a stone or marble top, very good. If not, do not despair. Pieces of slate or marble can be fastened to a thin sheet of wood cut to the size needed; glue felt or small rubber feet on the reverse side to avoid scratching. The stone top does not have to cover the entire altar. There are also marble cutting or pastry boards available which work nicely. These usually have rubber feet already on them.

Stone, and especially marble, is an excellent resonator of magical power. The more you use such an altar, the more power is stored in the stone. This can be drawn off to amplify your own power for spellworking.

For spellworking, place your altar so that you face the north. Later, when you have more experience and if you so desire, you can change the altar to face the direction that corresponds to the type of magic you will be doing. Gather as many representative articles as you can to help. See the Tables of Correspondence for aid in this.

A robe used only for magic helps the subconscious mind make the transition from everyday working to magical working. So does any special jewelry, such as an arm-band, bracelet, or amulet. It is now possible to purchase small pendants of Thorr's hammer. Or you might wish to wear a piece of amber on a chain. If you plan to do any outside work, a dark blue or black hooded cape is nice to have for cold weather.

If you want the more authentic-looking garb of a Norse rune-master, men can wear trousers with a long overtunic and women a long skirt with long overtunic. Both wear leather boots or slippers, a leather belt with a knife sheath and pouches for runestones and other magical supplies. A headband embroidered or painted with runes completes the outfit.

In selecting a dagger, try to purchase a new, double-edged knife that has a blade no longer than your palm and fingers. Used knives too often have negative vibrations that can sometimes be impossible to purge. Swords should not be too heavy or long. Holding a sword out in front of you for five minutes can play havoc with the neck and shoulder muscles if it is too awkward and heavy.

It is a Norse tradition to name daggers and swords. Take your time choosing such a name, then carve or paint it in runes on the hilt, along with the magical name you have chosen for yourself. For the correct runes, see the chapter on Spellwork.

The goblet can be of any material. However, if you choose one of brass, bronze, pewter, etc., be certain that it is lined with silver. This prevents wine and other acidic beverages from causing a dangerous reaction with the metal. A drinking horn is nice, and they are becoming easier to find. The horn should have a stand so that balancing it on the altar does not become a juggling feat.

Incense burners are common. A burner with chains is a must if you plan to carry it around the circle. Place a layer of sand in your burner to make cleaning easier and to cut down on the heat. The cauldron is generally of black cast iron with a bail and with or without feet. It does not have to be large. The small offering bowl and plate should also be of a non-flammable material.

The altar candles used for lighting are generally white or black. Set one at each end of the altar so you can see clearly. The holders should be wide enough to catch melting wax and be non-flammable, of course.

Wands are usually not longer than your forearm. A long wand does not increase the magical power; it merely becomes awkward. You can make your wands from specific types of trees. Remember to ask the tree's permission before cutting any branches, and always leave a gift of milk and honey. If you do not have access to such branches, you can make your wands out of wooden dowels and decorate them to suit yourself. I have never found that expensive silver wands worked any better than those of wood. Having more than one wand makes it possible to designate specific uses to each one, but more than one wand is not really necessary.

Your herb supplies should be kept in sealed containers in a cool, dry place out of sunlight. This helps to retain their freshness and potency longer. Use glass or earthenware containers, never metal.

The small bell and horn for blowing are not mandatory but do help in certain spellworkings. If at all possible, the horn should be a natural one, made of a hollowed cow's horn.

If you plan to do cord magic, purchase several 12-18 inch lengths of narrow round cording in various colors. White is used for spiritual undertakings and truth; black for binding, reversing and protection; red for energy or physical love; pink for pure love, romance and togetherness. Green is used for prosperity, fertility, marriage and growth; blue for healing, wisdom, understanding and peace. Orange is for changing luck, attracting good things and control; yellow for intellect, imagination, persuasion and concentration. The color purple is for permanent changes in life, psychic development, protection and breaking bad luck. Use white or purple when you are uncertain what color to use. Thread in these same colors is useful when spellwork calls for you to dispose of the knotted cord.

Anytime you are asking the Light Elves and Good Dwarves to work with you, you will need certain stones to entice them. Use quartz or rock crystal and moonstone for the Elves; steel or iron and pyrite (fool's gold) for the Dwarves.

Runestones can be purchased, or you can make your own with very little trouble. You can cut flat, thin pieces of wood into one-inch squares and paint or burn the runes on one side only. Small flat stones, also no more than one inch across, can be painted with the runes. If you want to be elaborate and have access to deer antlers, you can saw thin pieces of this material and paint on the runes. A piece of black cloth or short fur to use for throwing the runes is a nice touch.

Slowly acquire your tools, carefully choosing each to fit your vibrations. If a tool does not "feel" right, it is not for you. The important thing to remember is that the magic lies within *you,* not the tools. It can only be amplified through the implements. You and your subconscious mind are the originators of all magical power.

Carefully think out what you want to accomplish. Be certain that you are justified in the request. Taking someone's husband or wife, for instance, is bound to bring repercussions that you may not want or be able to handle.

Above all, relax and enjoy yourself. The whole idea in using Norse magic is to improve yourself and your life. Remember, magic works if you think it works.

7. Norse Wicca and the Lady

There are certain observances and beliefs which all Wiccan individuals and groups hold to be true, regardless of the deity names they choose to use. The Wiccan believe in a main Goddess (the Lady) and a main God (the Lord), with the Goddess having primary importance. They use certain symbols with a magical significance, such as the pentagram. They observe Moon phases in connection with spellworking. They celebrate eight yearly festivals and each Full Moon. And they believe in magic and its powers.

The Goddess is worshipped as a Triple Deity—Maiden, Mother and Crone (Dark Mother, Wise Woman, the Hag). In Norse mythology, the Goddess specifically called "the Lady" is Freyja. She is also called the Seer, the Great Goddess, Queen of the Valkyries. She is a Moon Goddess and a shape-shifter, the sister of Freyr and the daughter of Njord. As you would expect from a Norse Great Goddess, Freyja is independent, intelligent, and highly respected in Asgard.

The pentagram is one of Freyja's symbols. A pentagram is an ancient five-pointed star, with one upward point. Used in the reverse position in the U.S.A., it is a symbol of Satanists. The five points of the pentagram represent the four Elements plus Spirit. It was and is a favorite symbol of the Wiccan and magicians. Sometimes it is called a pentacle, although that word now means any disk of metal or wood that is engraved with a pentagram and magical symbols. The pentacle disk is placed on the altar as a power-point for consecrating objects, such as the water or wine in the chalice.

The Triple Goddess, or triple aspects of the Goddess, is represented by Idhunn as the Maiden, Freyja as the Mother, and Hel, Skadi or the German Holda/Bertha (another name for Hel) as the Crone or Dark Mother. The three-legged cauldron is a feminine symbol of the Triple Goddess.

Idhunn is the keeper of the golden apples of immortality. When she and her apples were stolen, the Gods of Asgard began to wither and age. As the Maiden, Idhunn was and is essential to the continuing of all life. Her color is white. She is the springtime, eternal youth and vigor, the dawn, enchantment, seduction, the waxing Moon.

Freyja, as the Great Mother, is the nurturing force behind the life that Idhunn creates. She is the ripeness of womanhood, desired by all the Gods, Dwarves, and Giants. Several of the Norse stories involve some supernatural being trying to wed Freyja or at least sleep with her. The Mother is Summer, the day, mother and teacher of life, nourishing, fertility, the Full Moon. Her color is color of blood and the life force.

The Crone, or Dark Mother, is depicted by Hel or Skadi, but could just as well be the German Goddess Holda/Bertha. This aspect of the Goddess is the waning Moon, wisdom, Winter, night, counsel, the gateway to death and reincarnation. The Crone is often called the Hag, because she joins Odhinn, the Lord of the Hunt, on his wild ride across the night skies. Her color is black, the color of darkness where all life rests before being reborn.

The Norse God known as "the Lord" is Freyr, god of fertility and of Yule. He is also called "the Lover." Like the Maiden, Freyr represents life, growth and balance.

Thorr corresponds to the Mother as defender of both the Asa-Gods and humans. When three god pillars were raised in a Norse temple, Thorr stood in the middle in the place of honor with Freyr on one side and Odhinn on the other. Thorr was the friend and deity of common humans.

Odhinn, known as the Great Father or Allfather, is the male equivalent of the Crone. He is wisdom gained through suffering and experience, as told in the story of how he gained knowledge of the runes. He is the Lord of the Wild Hunt, the authority over the Valkyries, the Avenger and ultimate Master in magic.

He and his brothers created the worlds listed in Norse mythology. During this creation, Odhinn sent four Dwarves to hold up the sky in the four directions. The four Dwarves correspond to the four Elements of Air, Fire, Water and Earth. One can call upon these four beings as Rulers of the Elements when casting the circle or spellworking in Norse magic.

The eight traditional Wiccan holy days are: Samhain, Winter Solstice, Imbolc, Spring Equinox, Beltane, Summer Solstice, Lunasa, and Autumn Equinox. Another holy day that easily could be celebrated in keeping with Norse ideas is the Feast of the Einheriar or Feast of the Fallen Warriors, which coincides with Veterans' Day.

The wheel is the symbol of the year with the Solstices and Equinoxes as the main spokes, the remaining four holy days as additional spokes.

The pagan year was based on lunar months, thus having thirteen months to a year. Beginning with the Full Moon closest to Winter Solstice, the Norse called these months: Wolf Moon; Snow Moon; Horning Moon; Plough Moon; Seed or Planting Moon; Hare Moon; Mead or Merry Moon; Fallow Moon; Corn Moon; Harvest Moon; Shedding Moon; Hunting Moon; Fog Moon.

Celebration of the solstices and equinoxes is done on a particular day when the Sun changes into particular zodiacal signs. This is listed on most calendars and varies from year to year. The remaining six holy days are honored by many Wiccan on a specific day also. However, I was taught differently. The present-day calendar has undergone at least one major change, and that heavily influenced by Christians. Therefore, I was told, the Wiccan should observe these four festivals on the nearest Full Moon of the correct sign. In the following discussions of these days, I will explain which Full Moon to use.

The ancient pagan world counted days as

starting at sunset. All their festivals were celebrated on the Eve, or night before. Therefore, Summer Solstice was celebrated on Midsummer's Eve, and so on.

The following seasonal holy day rituals are for the solitary practitioner. There is quite a lot of material available for groups, it seems to me, and more is needed for those pagans who wish to celebrate alone. If you have a partner, it is easy to divide the rituals so each has a part.

Samhain, pronounced *sow-en,* and called Halloween today, was the beginning of the Norse winter and probably was counted as the beginning of a new year. It was known as Ancestor Night, or Feast of the Dead. Because the Veil between the worlds is thinnest on this night, it was and is considered an excellent time for all types of divinations. Feasts are made in remembrance of past ancestors with the whole family or coven eating and drinking as an affirmation of continuing life. This is celebrated on the first Full Moon in Scorpio.

Winter Solstice, called Yule, occurs about December 21. This was known to the Norse as Jol (wheel) or Mother Night. This is the time of death and rebirth of the Sun God. The days are shortest, the Sun at its lowest point. The Triple Goddess rules with her aspect of the Crone ruling cold and darkness, and her aspect of the Mother giving birth to the Child of Promise. An oak Yule log (burned in honor of Thorr) is still a tradition in Norse/Germanic countries. The ashes are scattered over the fields, or the charred remains kept to start the next year's Yule log. Mistletoe was hung over the door to keep out malicious spirits. The same was done at Summer Solstice. The Full Moon after Yule is considered the most powerful of the whole year. The Yule ritual is always held indoors and is intensely personal, done only with family and coven members. Tradition says that if there was a knock on the door on this day, it wasn't answered. I suspect this was true on all pagan holy days to keep from being persecuted by the Christians. This ritual is a light festival, with as many candles as possible on or near the altar to welcome the Sun Child.

Imbolc is celebrated on the first Full Moon in Aquarius. It is a time of cleansing and purification, the root of the spring cleaning idea. It is a festival of the Maiden in preparation for growth and renewal.

Spring Equinox, about March 21, is a time of sowing in the North. Light and darkness are in balance, but the light is growing stronger. The Germanic peoples lit bonfires and jumped over the embers, or drove cattle between two bonfires for fertility.

Beltane is the first Full Moon in Taurus. It is called *Walpurgisnacht* by the Germans; other names for it are May Day or Lady Day. This festival is dedicated to "the Bright One," god of light and fire, or Balder the Sun God. In the Northlands, cattle were taken off to summer pastures right after this holy day. It is primarily a fertility festival with nature enchantments and offerings to wildlings and elementals. The powers of Elves and Fairies are growing and will reach their height at Summer Solstice. A time of great magic, it is good for all divinations and for establishing a woodland or garden shrine. The house guardians should be honored at this time.

Summer Solstice, about June 22, was called *Sonnenwende* (Sun's Turning) by the Germans. The Sun is at his highest before he begins his slide into darkness; the hours of daylight are longest. Bonfires are again lit and used as on Beltane *(Walpurgisnacht)*. The God-aspect as Fire and the Goddess-aspect as Water are balanced. In Scandinavia, the midsummer bonfires were called Balder's Balefires and symbolized his funeral pyre. Ashes from these were carried home for luck. The bonfires also were believed to drive off trolls and other malicious spirits. Mistletoe was also gathered and hung over doors to keep out such spirits. Traditionally, herbs gathered on this day are extremely powerful. On this night Elves and other ethereal beings are abroad in great numbers.

Lunasa is the first Full Moon in Leo. It is a corn or harvest festival, the turning point in Mother Earth's year, actually a preharvest festival except in the cold northern lands. The last herbs are gathered. On this holy day it is believed that the most fanciful desire can become reality.

Autumn Equinox, about September 21, was a time of rest after labor, completion of the harvest. Again the hours of day and night are in balance, with the darkness increasing. Thanks was given for the abundance stored for winter. All preparations for the dark of the year and the year's ending were made, thus bringing us back to Samhain.

SEASONAL RITUALS

Ancestor Night or
Feast of the Dead

(First Full Moon of Scorpio. Also called Samhain and Halloween.)

Special Notes: This is the Time of the Thin Veil or communion with the dead, the ruling time of the Crone. A "sacrificial" feast of cookies or cakes in animal and human shapes is appropriate.

Altar Supplies: incense, burner, chalice of water, salt, pentacle, dagger or sword, 4 Element candles, cauldron, chalice of wine, plate of cookies, plate of bread and salt. You will need extra candles (two white, two red, two black) and holders for them. Arrange a white, red and black together on the left side of the altar and a white, red and black on the right side.

Cast the circle with the dagger or sword, saying:

> *I consecrate this circle of power to the
>   Ancient Gods.*
> *Here may they manifest and bless their
>   child.*

Go back to the altar, facing north, and raise your hand or wand in greeting. Say:

> *This is a time that is not a time, in a
>   place that is not a place, on a day that
>   is not a day.*
> *I stand at the threshold between the
>   worlds, before the Gates of Asgard.*

> *May the Ancient Ones help and protect*
> *me on my magical journey.*

Set the chalice of water on the pentacle. Hold your dagger over the chalice, saying:

> *Great Goddess Freyja, bless this crea-*
> *ture of Water to your service.*
> *May we always remember the cauldron*
> *waters of rebirth.*

Hold your dagger over the salt, saying:

> *Great Goddess Freyja, bless this crea-*
> *ture of Earth to your service.*
> *May we always honor the blessed Earth,*
> *its many forms and beings.*

Sprinkle a little salt into the water, then hold the chalice up high. Say:

> *Great Freyja, be you adored!*

Sprinkle the water mixture lightly around the edges of the circle, moving clockwise and beginning in the east. Replace the chalice on the altar. Hold your dagger over the incense burner, saying:

> *Great God Freyr, bless this creature of*
> *Fire to your service.*
> *May we always remember the sacred*
> *Fire that dances within the form of*
> *every creation.*

Hold your dagger over the incense, saying:

> *Great God Freyr, bless this creature of*
> *Air to your service.*
> *May we always listen to the spirit winds*

> *that bring us the voices of the Ancient
> Ones.*

Put a little incense on the charcoal and, using the chains, briefly touch the burner to the pentacle, then raise the burner high, saying:

> *Great Freyr, be you adored!*

Carry the burner around the circle clockwise, beginning in the east. Return it to the altar.

Light the yellow candle in the east and say:

> *I call upon you, Powers of Air, to witness
> this rite and to guard this circle.*

Light the red candle in the south and say:

> *I call upon you, Powers of Fire, to wit-
> ness this rite and to guard this circle.*

Light the blue candle in the west and say:

> *I call upon you, Powers of Water, to wit-
> ness this rite and to guard this circle.*

Finally, light the green candle in the north and say:

> *I call upon you, Powers of Earth, to wit-
> ness this rite and to guard this circle.*

Move back to the altar, face north and raise your arms in greeting:

> *This circle is bound,*
> *With power all around.*
> *Within it I stand*
> *With protection at hand.*

Turn to the three candles on the left side of

the altar, saying:

> *I light three candles for the God-
> dess...as Maiden, as Mother, as Wise
> One.* (Light the white.) *Glorious Id-
> hunn, keeper of the golden apples,
> forever the Maiden of youth and new be-
> ginnings, dawn and the planted seed.*
> (Light the red.) *Lovely Freyja, Great
> Mother of magic and plenty, love and
> knowledge.* (Light the black.) *Dark
> Mother Hel, wise one of the twilight
> lands; queen of the night, death and re-
> birth. I welcome the Goddess in all her
> forms.*

Turn to the three candles on the right side of
the altar, saying:

> *I light three candles for the God...as
> Lover, as Warrior, as Allfather.* (Light
> the white.) *Bright Freyr, Father of love,
> skill and plenty, the bright day and suc-
> cess.* (Light the red.) *Mighty Thorr,
> warrior and defender, skilled in battle.*
> (Light the black.) *Dark Odhinn,
> Allfather, ruler of the Gods and men. I
> welcome the God in all his forms.*

Raise your arms and say:

> *This is Ancestor Night, the Feast of
> the Dead, the night of the wheel-
> turning year that brings us to the Thin
> Veil. The gates between the worlds stand
> open this night. The footsteps of my an-
> cestors rustle in the fallen leaves. The*

whispering winds carry their voices to me. All those who wish me well are welcomed within this circle.

Place the plate of bread and salt on the pentacle:

This is Ancestor Night, the Feast of the Dead, the night strongest for communication with those gone into the shadow lands, those who now dwell over Bifrost, the Rainbow Bridge to Asgard. The Veil has been lifted that I may know I am not forgotten, that I may hear the voices of my ancestors. All those who wish me well are welcomed within this circle.

Take the plate of bread and salt and hold it up before you. Say:

May I always have good health, prosperity and plenty.

Dip a piece of the bread into the salt and eat it. Set the plate aside and put the wine chalice on the pentacle, with the plate of cookies next to it:

I ask all who have gathered here to join me in this feast.

Take up the cup of wine and say:

May I always be strong in body,
     mind and spirit.
To the Gods of Asgard!
Merry meet and merry part and merry
     meet again.

Drink some of the wine and eat some of the cookies, saving some back to be put outside later for the nature spirits. (Always save some of your wine and ritual feast to be placed outside for the "little people".) Replace the wine chalice on the altar.

Turn back to the Goddess candles or an image of her. Say:

> The year wheel has turned, the harvest has come again. I have sowed many thought-seeds since last Ancestor Night. Let the good be harvested; let those that would hinder or hurt me be cast aside. The Threefold Goddess—the Maiden, the Mother, the Wise One—has covered me with her gentle hands, guided my steps, heard my desires. For this I give her honor and love.

Turn to the God candles or an image of him. Say:

> The year wheel has turned, the harvest has come again. Once more I stand before the Thin Veil, before the gates that divide the worlds. The Great God, the Warrior of the night skies, has protected me with his sword and hammer, guided my steps, heard my desires. For this I give him honor and love.

Tap the pentacle gently with your wand, saying:

> Give me the true inner vision. Hear my desires, O Great Ones! Guide and

*protect me. Lead me to greater knowl-
edge and fulfillment.*

Stand in silence while you ask what you need
of the Gods. When finished, say:

*All love and honor to the Great Lady
and her Lord. Blessed be!*

Now is a time for divination, meditation, or
spellwork. If any spellworking is done, finish with:

*By the powers of the ancient Gods,
I bind all power within this circle
Into this spell. So mote it be!*

Extinguish the eastern candle and say:

*Depart in peace, O Powers of Air.
My thanks and blessings.*

Extinguish the southern candle and say:

*Depart in peace, O Powers of Fire.
My thanks and blessings.*

Extinguish the western candle and say:

*Depart in peace, O Powers of Water.
My thanks and blessings.*

Finally, extinguish the northern candle and
say:

*Depart in peace, O Powers of Earth.
My thanks and blessings.*

Return to the altar, raise your arms and say:

*To all beings and powers of the visible
and invisible, depart in peace.
May there always be harmony between*

us.
My thanks and blessings.

Cut the circle to end the ritual. Say:

The circle is open, yet ever it remains a
circle.
Around and through me always flows
its magical power.

Be sure to put out your offering for the nature
spirits.

Yule or Mother Night

(About December 21. Also called Winter Solstice.)

Special Notes: Time of the Goddess of the Cold Darkness and the birth of the Divine Child, the reborn Sun God. The Triple Goddess rules. A time of rebirth and turning of the earth force tides.

Altar Supplies: incense, burner, chalice of water, salt, pentacle, chalice of wine, dagger or sword, bell. Green candle in the cauldron with a red, a white, and a black candle arranged around it.

Cast the circle with the dagger or sword, saying:

> *I consecrate this circle of power to the Ancient Gods.*
> *Here may they manifest and bless their child.*

Go back to the altar, facing north, and raise your hand or wand in greeting. Say:

> *This is a time that is not a time, in a place that is not a place, on a day that is not a day.*
> *I stand at the threshold between the worlds, before the Gates of Asgard.*
> *May the Ancient Ones help and protect me on my magical journey.*

Set the chalice of water on the pentacle. Hold your dagger over the chalice, saying:

> *Great Goddess Freyja, bless this creature of Water to your service.*

> *May we always remember the cauldron
> waters of rebirth.*

Hold your dagger over the salt, saying:

> *Great Goddess Freyja, bless this crea-
> ture of Earth to your service.*
> *May we always honor the blessed Earth,
> its many forms and beings.*

Sprinkle a little salt into the water, then hold
the chalice up high. Say:

> *Great Freyja, be you adored!*

Sprinkle the water mixture lightly around
the edges of the circle, moving clockwise and beginning in the east. Replace the chalice on the altar. Hold your dagger over the incense burner, saying:

> *Great God Freyr, bless this creature of
> Fire to your service.*
> *May we always remember the sacred
> Fire that dances within the form of
> every creation.*

Hold your dagger over the incense, saying:

> *Great God Freyr, bless this creature of
> Air to your service.*
> *May we always listen to the spirit winds
> that bring us the voices of the Ancient
> Ones.*

Put a little incense on the charcoal and, using
the chains, briefly touch the burner to the pentacle, then raise the burner high saying:

> *Great Freyr, be you adored!*

Carry the burner around the circle clockwise, beginning in the east. Return it to the altar.

Light the yellow candle in the east and say:

I call upon you, Powers of Air, to witness this rite and to guard this circle.

Light the red candle in the south and say:

I call upon you, Powers of Fire, to witness this rite and to guard this circle.

Light the blue candle in the west and say:

I call upon you, Powers of Water, to witness this rite and to guard this circle.

Finally, light the green candle in the north and say:

I call upon you, Powers of Earth, to witness this rite and to guard this circle.

Move back to the altar, face north and raise your arms in greeting:

This circle is bound,
With power all around.
Within it I stand
With protection at hand.

Ring the bell three times. Say:

This is the night of Yule, the Winter Solstice, the longest night of the year. Darkness reigns triumphant, yet gives way and changes into light. The breath of all nature is suspended, while within the cauldron of rebirth the Dark King is transformed into the newborn Infant

Light.

Put a little more incense on the coals:

The season of life is past and all is cold. I await the coming of dawn, when the Triple Goddess once more gives birth to the Divine Child, the Sun King. I stand in the stillness behind all motion, before the cauldron of rebirth, knowing that someday I too must pass through the cauldron and be reborn. I now give honor to the Triple Goddess that the season may be made better through her Divine Child.

Light the white candle near the cauldron:

White is for Idhunn, the Maiden. May you plant your seeds of joy and new beginnings within my life.

Light the red candle near the cauldron:

Red is for Freyja, the Mother. From you I ask the gifts of creative ideas and the strength to bring them to completion.

Light the black candle near the cauldron:

Black is for Hel (Skadi or Holda), the Wise One. I ask of you the wisdom to understand the magical mysteries.

Light the green candle within the cauldron:

Green is for the newborn Lord of the forests, the Divine Sun Child, the god of many forms, and consort of the Goddess. I welcome you again into life.

Take the bell and go to the east. Ring the bell once:

Greet the Divine Child, O Powers of Air. Blow upon him with your gentle breezes.

Go to the south and ring the bell once:

Greet the Divine Child, O Powers of Fire. Warm him with your tender sunbeams.

Go the the west and ring the bell once:

Greet the Divine Child, O Powers of Water. Bless him with your spring showers.

Go to the north and ring the bell once:

Greet the Divine Child, O Powers of Earth. Cradle him with flowers and soft green boughs.

Go back to the altar and stand facing north. Ring the bell three times:

Hail, O God of the woodlands and new life! I give you honor and ask your blessing.

Stand in silence to receive the blessing. Ring the bell again three times:

Hail, Triple Goddess, the three in one, bringer of light out of darkness and new life out of the cauldron of rebirth. I give you honor and ask your blessing.

Again stand in silence to receive the blessing.

Place the wine chalice on the pentacle for a few moments, then lift it high, saying:

> *To the Gods of Asgard! Merry meet and*
> *merry part and merry meet again.*

Drink the wine, saving some back to be put outside for the nature spirits.

Now is a time for divination, meditation, or spellwork. If any spellworking is done, finish with:

> *By the powers of the ancient Gods,*
> *I bind all power within this circle*
> *Into this spell. So mote it be!*

Extinguish the eastern candle and say:

> *Depart in peace, O Powers of Air.*
> *My thanks and blessings.*

Extinguish the southern candle and say:

> *Depart in peace, O Powers of Fire.*
> *My thankss and blessings.*

Extinguish the western candle and say:

> *Depart in peace, O Powers of Water.*
> *My thanks and blessings.*

Finally, extinguish the northern candle and say:

> *Depart in peace, O Powers of Earth.*
> *My thanks and blessings.*

Return to the altar, raise your arms and say:

> *To all beings and powers of the visible*
> *and invisible, depart in peace.*
> *May there always be harmony between*

us.
My thanks and blessings.

Cut the circle to end the ritual. Say:

The circle is open, yet ever it remains a
*   circle.*
Around and through me always flows its
*   magical power.*

Be sure to put out your offering for the nature
spirits.

Imbolc

(First Full Moon of Aquarius. Also called Im-
bolg and Candlemas.)

Special Notes: First stirrings of Mother
Earth; spring cleaning; time of cleansing and purification; preparation for growth and renewal.

Altar Supplies: burner, incense, chalice of
water, salt, pentacle, chalice of wine, dagger or
sword. White candle in cauldron with a red candle
on the left and a green candle on the right.

Cast the circle with the dagger or sword, saying:

> *I consecrate this circle of power to the*
>   *Ancient Gods.*
> *Here may they manifest and bless their*
>   *child.*

Go back to the altar, facing north, and raise
your hand or wand in greeting. Say:

> *This is a time that is not a time, in a*
>   *place that is not a place, on a day that*
>   *is not a day.*
> *I stand at the threshold between the*
>   *worlds, before the Gates of Asgard.*
> *May the Ancient Ones help and protect*
>   *me on my magical journey.*

Set the chalice of water on the pentacle. Hold
your dagger over the chalice, saying:

> *Great Goddess Freyja, bless this crea-*
>   *ture of Water to your service.*
> *May we always remember the cauldron*

waters of rebirth.

Hold your dager over the salt, saying:

*Great Goddess Freyja, bless this crea-
ture of Earth to your service.
May we always honor the blessed Earth,
its many forms and beings.*

Sprinkle a little salt into the water, then hold
the chalice up high. Say:

Great Freyja, be you adored!

Sprinkle the water mixture lightly around
the edges of the circle, moving clockwise and beginning in the east. Replace the chalice on the altar. Hold your dagger over the incense burner, saying:

*Great God Freyr, bless this creature of
Fire to your service.
May we always remember the sacred
Fire that dances within the form of
every creation.*

Hold your dagger over the incense, saying:

*Great God Freyr, bless this creature of
Air to your service.
May we always listen to the spirit winds
that bring us the voices of the Ancient
Ones.*

Put a little incense on the charcoal and, using
the chains, briefly touch the burner to the pentacle, then raise the burner high, saying:

Great Freyr, be you adored!

Carry the burner around the circle clockwise, beginning in the east. Return it to the altar.

Light the yellow candle in the east and say:

I call upon you, Powers of Air, to witness this rite and to guard this circle.

Light the red candle in the south and say:

I call upon you, Powers of Fire, to witness this rite and to guard this circle.

Light the blue candle in the west and say:

I call upon you, Powers of Water, to witness this rite and to guard this circle.

Finally, light the green candle in the north and say:

I call upon you, Powers of Earth, to witness this rite and to guard this circle.

Move back to the altar, face north and raise your arms in greeting:

This circle is bound,
With power all around.
Within it I stand.
With protection at hand.

Add a little more incense to the burner, then say:

I greet thee, Mother Earth, as you awaken from your long slumber. I join with my distant ancestors in giving honor to the Ancient Ones. Prepare the fields and forests, all creatures who inhabit your realms, for the coming of habit your realms, for the coming of spring.

Tap the altar three times with your wand, dagger or sword:

This is the feast of waxing light. It is a time of initiation, of purification, a renewed promise of the Lady and her Lord for the future. At this time and in this place I prepare my thought-seeds for the future.

(Time of silence while you ask the Lord and Lady for inspiration and guidance for the future.)

Tap the altar again gently three times:

O Ancient Ones, I give my dreams into your keeping. For only with your guidance and help may I see these dream-seeds grow into reality.

Light the white candle in the cauldron:

At this time and in this place do I salute the noble Goddess as the sacred Maiden, now returned from the darkness. Preparation for new life begins as she spreads her blessings upon all the land and her children.

Light the red candle on the left of the cauldron:

Behold, the Earth feels the first stirrings of the Goddess. From her realm in the marsh-halls, Freyja smiles upon the Earth and all things begin regeneration.

*As there is renewal within the plants
and animals, so should there be renewal
in my own life. Great Goddess Freyja, I
ask for insight, good health, prosperity
and magical power.*

Light the green candle on the right of the
cauldron:

*Behold, the God approaches the
dreaming Earth, beckoning her back
into fertility with his power and
thought. The year wheel turns again towards spring. Mighty glorious Freyr, in-
spire me to new goals. Make my life fer-
tile with insight, good health, prosperity
and magical power.*

Place the wine chalice on the pentacle for a
few moments, then lift it high, saying:

*To the Gods of Asgard! Merry meet and
merry part and merry meet again.*

Drink the wine, saving some back to be put
outside for the nature spirits.

Now is a time for divination, meditation, or
spellwork. If any spellworking is done, finish with:

*By the powers of the ancient Gods,
I bind all powers within this circle
Into this spell. So mote it be!*

Extinguish the eastern candle and say:

*Depart in peace, O Powers of Air.
My thanks and blessings.*

Extinguish the southern candle and say:

Depart in peace, O Powers of Fire.
My thanks and blessings.

Extinguish the western candle and say:

Depart in peace, O Powers of Water.
My thanks and blessings.

Finally, extinguish the northern candle and say:

Depart in peace, O Powers of Earth.
My thanks and blessings.

Return to the altar, raise your arms and say:

To all beings and powers of the visible
*   and invisible, depart in peace.*
May there always be harmony between
*   us.*
My thanks and blessings.

Cut the circle to end the ritual. Say:

The circle is open, yet ever it remains a
*   circle.*
Around and through me always flows its
*   magical power.*

Be sure to put out your offering for the nature spirits.

Spring Equinox

(About March 21. Also called Summer Finding. Roughly corresponds to the Christian Easter.)

Special Notes: Sowing time in the north; Earth cycle of plant and animal fertility, spell producing, new beginnings. Balance of light and dark. The decorated egg is an appropriate symbol of renewing life.

Altar Supplies: burner, incense, chalice of water, salt, pentacle, chalice of wine, dagger or sword, wand, cauldron with red candle, dish for burning, parchment and pen, bell. Colored eggs and spring flowers for decorations.

Cast the circle with the dagger or sword, saying:

> I consecrate this circle of power to the
>   Ancient Gods.
> Here may they manifest and bless their
>   child.

Go back to the altar, facing north, and raise your hand or wand in greeting. Say:

> This is a time that is not a time, in a
>   place that is not a place, on a day that
>   is not a day.
> I stand at the threshold between the
>   worlds, before the Gates of Asgard.
> May the Ancient Ones help and protect
>   me on my magical journey.

Set the chalice of water on the pentacle. Hold your dagger over the chalice, saying:

> Great Goddess Freyja, bless this crea-

> ture of Water to your service.
> May we always remember the cauldron
>   waters of rebirth.

Hold your dagger over the salt, saying:

> Great Goddess Freyja, bless this crea-
>   ture of Earth to your service.
> May we always honor the blessed Earth,
>   its many forms and beings.

Sprinkle a little salt into the water, then hold the chalice up high. Say:

> Great Freyja, be you adored!

Sprinkle the water mixture lightly around the edges of the circle, moving clockwise and beginning in the east. Replace the chalice on the altar. Hold your dagger over the incense burner, saying:

> Great God Freyr, bless this creature of
>   Fire to your service.
> May we always remember the sacred
>   Fire that dances within the form of
>   every creation.

Hold your dagger over the incense, saying:

> Great God Freyr, bless this creature of
>   Air to your service.
> May we always listen to the spirit winds
>   that bring us the voices of the Ancient
>   Ones.

Put a little incense on the charcoal and, using the chains, briefly touch the burner to the pentacle, then raise the burner high, saying:

Great Freyr, be you adored!

Carry the burner around the circle clockwise, beginning in the east. Return it to the altar.

Light the yellow candle in the east and say:

*I call upon you, Powers of Air, to witness
this rite and to guard this circle.*

Light the red candle in the south and say:

*I call upon you, Powers of Fire, to wit-
ness this rite and to guard this circle.*

Light the blue candle in the west and say:

*I call upon you, Powers of Water, to wit-
ness this rite and to guard this circle.*

Finally, light the green candle in the north and say:

*I call upon you, Powers of Earth, to wit-
ness this rite and to guard this circle.*

Move back to the altar, face north and raise your arms in greeting:

*This circle is bound,
With power all around.
Within it I stand
With protection at hand.*

Pick up your wand and raise your arms in greeting again, say:

*Behold, the God, Lord of death and
resurrection, of life and the giver of life.
Without her Lord, the Goddess is bar-
ren. Without his Lady, the God has no*

*life. Each is needful of the other for com-
pletion and power, as Sun to Earth, the
spear to the cauldron, spirit to flesh,
man to woman.*

Rap the cauldron lightly with the wand and
say:

*O Goddess of the Earth, be with me
now as Idhunn, the Maiden, the fair one
who brings joy and new life.*

Ring the bell once and say:

*O God of renewal, be with me now as
Freyr, the Lover, the laughing one who
brings warmth and love.*

Rap the cauldron once more with the wand.

*May the strength of the old enter into
the new. O Ancient Ones, make all
things strong and giving of new life.
Blessed be!*

Put a little incense on the coals and carry the
burner again around the circle clockwise. Put it
back on the altar and raise your arms, saying:

*Harken to me! Awake! It is time to
greet the spring. Idhunn, Maiden of
Light, hear me! Freyr, Lord of Life, hear
me!*

Touch the parchment paper with the dagger
or sword, saying:

*Now I cast behind me the darkness of
winter and the past, and look forward to
that which lies ahead. Now is the time*

for the planting of seeds in the physical,
mental and spiritual realms.

Write on the parchment your desires for the coming year. Fold the papers and hold them up over the altar:

This is a joyous time, a time for planting.

Light the papers from the cauldron candle and drop them into the burning dish:

These seeds do I place in the realms of
the Ancient Gods of Asgard, that these
desires and dreams may manifest and
become a part of my life. Blessed be the
Gods!

Place the wine chalice on the pentacle for a few moments, then lift it high, saying:

To the Gods of Asgard! Merry meet and
merry part and merry meet again.

Drink the wine, saving some back to be put outside for the nature spirits.

Now is a time for divination, meditation, or spellwork. If any spellworking is done, finish with:

By the powers of the ancient Gods,
I bind all power within this circle
Into this spell. So mote it be!

Extinguish the eastern candle and say:

Depart in peace, O Powers of Air.
My thanks and blessings.

Extinguish the southern candle and say:

Depart in peace, O Powers of Fire.

My thanks and blessings.

Extinguish the western candle and say:

Depart in peace, O Powers of Water.
My thanks and blessings.

Finally, extinguish the northern candle and say:

Depart in peace, O Powers of Earth.
My thanks and blessings.

Return to the altar, raise your arms and say:

To all beings and powers of the visible
  and invisible, depart in peace.
May there always be harmony between
  us.
My thanks and blessings.

Cut the circle to end the ritual. Say:

The circle is open, yet ever it remains a
  circle.
Around and through me always flows its
  magical power.

Be sure to put out your offering for the nature spirits.

Walpurgisnacht

(First Full Moon of Taurus. Also called Lady Day, May Day and Beltane.)

Special Notes: Time of the Horned God and the Lady of the Greenwood; honor of the house guardian.

Altar Supplies: burner, incense, chalice of water, salt, pentacle, chalice of wine, dagger or sword, wand. Somewhere within the circle area, the house guardian or his symbol, in whatever form you have chosen; along with perfumed oil.

Cast the circle with the dagger or sword, saying:

> *I consecrate this circle of power to the Ancient Gods.*
>
> *Here may they manifest and bless their child.*

Go back to the altar, facing north, and raise your hand or wand in greeting. Say:

> *This is a time that is not a time, in a place that is not a place, on a day that is not a day.*
> *I stand at the threshold between the worlds, before the Gates of Asgard.*
> *May the Ancient Ones help and protect me on my magical journey.*

Set the chalice of water on the pentacle. Hold your dagger over the chalice, saying:

> *Great Goddess Freyja, bless this creature of Water to your service.*

*May we always remember the cauldron
waters of rebirth.*

Hold your dagger over the salt, saying:

*Great Goddess Freyja, bless this crea-
ture of Earth to your service.
May we always honor the blessed Earth,
its many forms and beings.*

Sprinkle a little salt into the water, then hold
the chalice up high. Say:

Great Freyja, be you adored!

Sprinkle the water mixture lightly around
the edges of the circle, moving clockwise and beginning in the east. Replace the chalice on the altar. Hold your dagger over the incense burner, saying:

*Great God Freyr, bless this creature of
Fire to your service.
May we always remember the sacred
Fire that dances within the form of
every creation.*

Hold your dagger over the incense, saying:

*Great God Freyr, bless this creature of
Air to your service.
May we always listen to the spirit winds
that bring us the voices of the Ancient
Ones.*

Put a little incense on the charcoal and, using
the chains, briefly touch the burner to the pentacle, then raise the burner high, saying:

Great Freyr, be you adored!

Carry the burner around the circle clockwise, beginning in the east. Return it to the altar.

Light the yellow candle in the east and say:

I call upon you, Powers of Air, to witness this rite and to guard this circle.

Light the red candle in the south and say:

I call upon you, Powers of Fire, to witness this rite and to guard this circle.

Light the blue candle in the west and say:

I call upon you, Powers of Water, to witness this rite and to guard this circle.

Finally, light the green candle in the north and say:

I call upon you, Powers of Earth, to witness this rite and to guard this circle.

Move back to the altar, face north and raise your arms in greeting:

This circle is bound,
With power all around.
Within it I stand
With protection at hand.

Raise your wand in greeting, say:

I do call the Goddess to be here with me, she once called "the Lady of May." Greetings, O Goddess of things wild, of trees, of skies, and of waters. Blessed be.

Dance around the altar, beginning in the east, and moving clockwise. Pause to salute each element with raised arms. Move back to the altar when finished.

> *I am the servant, thou the Lady. I am
> the hands to obey, the weapon to use, the
> body to serve. I was born to thy service,
> and by thy will shall I live, to die at the
> time appointed. Let now thy great light
> come into me. I am a cup to be filled, that
> I may do what is needful. Blessed be thy
> commands. Let my ears hear them, my
> hands and feet obey. Blessed be ever thy
> will which moves me.*

Stand before the house guardian or symbol.

> *Lovely Lady, great Lord, I present to
> you the guardian(s) of this house, the
> special spirit(s) I have invited into my
> home. I honor them in this symbol of
> their being. Great Freyr, lovely Freyja,
> bless this (these) guardian(s) of this
> house. And to your blessings, I add my
> thanks for their protection. Blessed be.*

The guardian symbol or statue is lightly
anointed with perfumed oil. If the symbol is such
that it cannot be oiled, at least swing the smoking
incense burner around it.

Place the wine chalice on the pentacle for a
few moments, then lift it high, saying:

> *To the Gods of Asgard! Merry meet and
> merry part and merry meet again.*

Drink the wine, saving some back to be put
outside for the nature spirits.

Now is a time for divination, meditation, or
spellwork. If any spellworking is done, finish with:

By the powers of the ancient Gods,
I bind all power within this circle
Into this spell. So mote it be!

Rap the altar three times with the wand, say:

As woods and meadows blossom and
green, I celebrate this ancient rite as the
old ones did before me. I cast my words
into the mists of time and space: Where I
stand now, in years to come, may scores
of other pagans be. So mote it be.

Extinguish the eastern candle and say:

Depart in peace, O Powers of Air.
My thanks and blessings.

Extinguish the southern candle and say:

Depart in peace, O Powers of Fire.
My thanks and blessings.

Extinguish the western candle and say:

Depart in peace, O Powers of Water.
My thanks and blessings.

Finally, extinguish the northern candle and
say:

Depart in peace, O Powers of Earth.
My thanks and blessings.

Return to the altar, raise your arms and say:

To all beings and powers of the visible
and invisible, depart in peace.
May there always be harmony between
us.
My thanks and blessings.

Cut the circle to end the ritual. Say:

The circle is open, yet ever it remains a circle
Around and through me always flows its magical power.

Be sure to put out your offering for the nature spirits.

Sonnenwende or Sun's Turning

(About June 22. Also called Summer Solstice.)

Special Notes: A Fire festival honoring the Sun God and the Water Goddess. Rededication to the Lord and the Lady.

Altar Supplies: burner, incense, chalice of water, salt, pentacle, chalice of wine, dagger or sword, wand. A red candle (set to the right of the cauldron) and a cup of fresh water set in the cauldron with a green or blue candle on the left.

Cast the circle with the dagger or sword, saying:

> I consecrate this circle of power to the
>   Ancient Gods.
> Here may they manifest and bless their
>   child.

Go back to the altar, facing north, and raise your hand or wand in greeting. Say:

> This is a time that is not a time, in a
>   place that is not a place, on a day that
>   is not a day.
> I stand at the threshold between the
>   worlds, before the Gates of Asgard.
> May the Ancient Ones help and protect
>   me on my magical journey.

Set the chalice of water on the pentacle. Hold your dagger over the chalice, saying:

> Great Goddess Freyja, bless this crea-
>   ture of Water to your service.

*May we always remember the cauldron
    waters of rebirth.*

Hold your dagger over the salt, saying:

*Great Goddess Freyja, bless this crea-
    ture of Earth to your service.
May we always honor the blessed Earth,
    its many forms and beings.*

Sprinkle a little salt into the water, then hold
the chalice up high. Say:

Great Freyja, be you adored!

Sprinkle the water mixture lightly around
the edges of the circle, moving clockwise and beginning in the east. Replace the chalice on the altar. Hold your dagger over the incense burner,
saying:

*Great God Freyr, bless this creature of
    Fire to your service.
May we always remember the sacred
    Fire that dances within the form of
    every creation.*

Hold your dagger over the incense, saying:

*Great God Freyr, bless this creature of
    Air to your service.
May we always listen to the spirit winds
    that bring us the voices of the Ancient
    Ones.*

Put a little incense on the charcoal and, using
the chains, briefly touch the burner to the pentacle, then raise the burner high, saying:

Great Freyr, be you adored!

Carry the burner around the circle clockwise, beginning in the east. Return it to the altar.

Light the yellow candle in the east and say:

I call upon you, Powers of Air, to witness
this rite and to guard this circle.

Light the red candle in the south and say:

I call upon you, Powers of Fire, to wit-
ness this rite and to guard this circle.

Light the blue candle in the west and say:

I call upon you, Powers of Water, to wit-
ness this rite and to guard this circle.

Finally, light the green candle in the north and say:

I call upon you, Powers of Earth, to wit-
ness this rite and to guard this circle.

Move back to the altar, face north and raise your arms in greeting:

This circle is bound,
With power all around.
Within it I stand
With protection at hand.

Light the green candle to the left of the cauldron, say:

Green forest Mother, be with me here
in your fullness of life, I do ask. Great
One of the stars, spinner of fates, I give
honor to you, and call upon you in your
ancient names, known and unknown.

Light the red candle to the right of the cauldron, say:

Great Balder, power of the Sun, laughing Freyr, god of fertility and plenty, be here with me here, I do ask. Lift up your shining spear of Light to protect me. I give honor to you, and call upon you in your ancient names, known and unknown.

Raise your arms over the cauldron, say:

This is the cauldron of Freyja, the Triple Goddess. The touch of its consecrated water blesses, even as the Sun, the Lord of Life, arises in his strength in the sign of the waters of life.

Pass your hands and arms between the two candles, making wishes as you do so. Or set the candles on the floor and carefully, slowly walk between them. Dip the forefinger of your power hand into the cauldron water and touch your forehead, lips, and breast. Kneel before the altar say:

I will serve the Goddess and give reverence to the God. I am a pagan, a stone of the ancient circle, standing firmly based and balanced on Earth, yet open to the winds of the Gods, and enduring through time. May the Asa-Gods witness my words!

Place the wine chalice on the pentacle for a few moments, then lift it high saying:

To the Gods of Asgard! Merry meet and merry part and merry meet again.

Drink the wine, saving some back to be put outside for the nature spirits.

Now is a time for divination, meditation, or spellwork. If any spellworking is done, finish with:

By the powers of the ancient Gods,
I bind all power within this circle
Into this spell. So mote it be.

Extinguish the eastern candle and say:

Depart in peace, O Powers of Air.
My thanks and blessings.

Extinguish the Southern candle and say:

Depart in peace, O powers of Fire.
My thanks and blessings

Extinguish the western candle and say:

Depart in peace, O powers of Water.
My thanks and blessings.

Finally, extinguish the northern candle and say:

Depart in peace, O powers of Earth.
My thanks and blessings.

Return to the altar, raise your arms and say:

To all beings and powers of the visible
*   and invisible, depart in peace.*
May there always be harmony between
*   us.*
My thanks and blessings.

Cut the circle to end the ritual. Say:

The circle is open, yet ever it remains a

> circle.
> *Around and through me always flows its
>   magical powers.*

Be sure to put out your offering for the nature spirits.

Lunasa

(First Full Moon in Leo.)

Special Notes: The turning point in Mother Earth's year; a harvest festival in the northern lands. The waning God and the waxing Goddess. Spellwork for good fortune and abundance is especially appropriate.

Altar Supplies: burner, incense, chalice of water, salt, pentacle, chalice of wine, dagger or sword, wand, plate of bread. Fall flowers, ivy and leaves for decoration; cauldron with a yellow or orange candle in it.

Cast the circle with the dagger or sword, saying:

I consecrate this circle of power to the Ancient Gods.
Here may they manifest and bless their child.

Go back to the altar, facing north, and raise your hand or wand in greeting: Say:

This is a time that is not a time, in a place that is not a place, on a day that is not a day.
I stand at the threshold between the worlds, before the Gates of Asgard.
May the Ancient Ones help and protect me on my magical journey.

Set the chalice of water on the pentacle. Hold your dagger over the chalice, saying:

Great Goddess Freyja, bless this creature of Water to your service.

*May we always remember the cauldron
    waters of rebirth.*

Hold your dagger over the salt, saying:

*Great Goddess Freyja, bless this
    creature of Earth to your service.
May we always honor the blessed Earth,
    its many forms and beings.*

Sprinkle a little salt into the water, then hold
the chalice up high. Say:

Great Freyja, be you adored.

Sprinkle the water mixture lightly around
the edges of the circle, moving clockwise and beginning in the east. Replace the chalice on the altar. Hold your dagger over the incense burner, saying:

*Great God Freyr, bless this creature of
    Fire to your service*
*May we always remember the sacred
    Fire that dances within the form of
    every creature.*

Hold your dagger over the incense, saying:

*Great God Freyr, bless this creature of
    Air to your service.*
*May we always listen to the spirit winds
    that bring us the voices of the Ancient
    Ones.*

Put a little incense on the charcoal and, using
the chains, briefly touch the burner to the pentacle, then raise the burner high saying:

Great Freyr, be you adored.

Carry the burner around the circle clockwise, beginning in the east. Return it to the altar.

Light the yellow candle in the east and say:

I call upon you, Powers of Air, to witness this rite and to guard this circle.

Light the red candle in the south and say:

I call upon you, Powers of Fire to witness this rite and to guard this circle.

Light the blue candle in the west and say:

I call upon you, Powers of Water, to witness this rite and to guard this circle.

Finally, light the green candle in the north and say:

I call upon you, Powers of Earth to witness this rite and to guard this circle.

Move back to the altar, face north and raise your arms in greeting:

This circle is bound,
With power all around.
Within it I stand
With protection at hand.

Light the cauldron candle, say:

O Ancient Gods of Asgard, I do ask your presence here. For this is a time that is not a time, in a place that is not a place, on a day that is not a day, and I await you.

Set the plate of bread on the pentacle. Stand still and breathe deeply for a few moments. Concentrate upon the cleansing power of the breath and air. When you feel ready, say:

I have purified myself by breathing in the life force of the universe and expelling all evil from me.

Lift the plate of bread high, then set it back on the altar. Put the chalice of wine on the pentacle. Say:

I know that every seed, every grain is the record of ancient times, and a promise to all of what shall be. This bread represents life eternal through the cauldron of the Goddess.

Eat a piece of bread. Hold high the wine chalice, then set it back on the altar. Say:

As the grape undergoes change to become a sparkling wine, so by life's cauldron shall I undergo change. And as this wine can give man enchantment of the divine or sink him into the lower realms, so I do realize that all humans rise or fall as their will and strength decrees.

Drink some of the wine. Say:

As in the bread and wine, so it is with me. The mysteries of ancient times are with me still. May the Asa-Gods lay their blessings upon me, that this season of waning light and increasing darkness may not be heavy. Merry meet and

*merry part and merry meet again. So
mote it be!*

Now is a time for divination, meditation, or
spellwork. If any spellworking is done, finish with:

*By the powers of the ancient Gods,
I bind all power within this circle.
Into this spell. So mote it be!*

Extinguish the eastern candle and say:

*Depart in peace, O Powers of Air.
My thanks and blessings.*

Extinguish the southern candle and say:

*Depart in peace, O Powers of Fire.
My thanks and blessings.*

Extinguish the western candle and say:

*Depart in peace, O Powers of Water.
My thanks and blessings.*

Finally, extinguish the northern candle and
say:

*Depart in peace, O Powers of Earth.
My thanks and blessings.*

Return to the altar, raise your arms and say:

*To all beings and powers of the visible
    and invisible, depart in peace.
May there always be harmony between
    us.
My thanks and blessings.*

Cut the circle to end the ritual. Say:

The circle is open, yet ever it remains a

circle.
*Around and through me always flows its
    magical power.*

Be sure to put out your offering for the nature
spirits.

Autumn Equinox

(About September 21. Also called Winter Finding.)

Special Notes: Balance of light and dark. Time of rest after labor, completion of the harvest, thanksgiving. A good time for meditations on reincarnations in preparation for Ancestor Night.

Altar Supplies: burner, incense, chalice of water, salt, pentacle, chalice of wine, dagger or sword, wand; autumn-colored ribbons tied on the dagger. Autumn leaves for decoration. Three candles (red, white, black) set around cauldron. Ivy in the cauldron.

Cast the circle with the dagger or sword, saying:

*I consecrate this circle of power to the
    Ancient Gods.
Here may they manifest and bless their
    child.*

Go back to the altar, facing north, and raise your hand or wand in greeting. Say:

*This is a time that is not a time, in a
    place that is not a place, on a day that
    is not a day.
I stand at the threshold between the
    worlds, before the Gates of Asgard.
May the Ancient Ones help and protect
    me on my magical journey.*

Set the chalice of water on the pentacle. Hold your dagger over the chalice, saying:

Great Goddess Freyja, bless this crea-

93

> ture of Water to your service.
> May we always remember the cauldron
>   waters of rebirth.

Hold your dagger over the salt, saying:

> Great Goddess Freyja, bless this crea-
>   ture of Earth to your service.
> May we always honor the blessed Earth,
>   its many forms and beings.

Sprinkle a little salt into the water, then hold
the chalice up high. Say:

> Great Freyja, be you adored!

Sprinkle the water mixture lightly around
the edges of the circle, moving clockwise and beginning in the east. Replace the chalice on the altar. Hold your dagger over the incense burner, saying:

> Great God Freyr, bless this creature of
>   Fire to your service.
> May we always remember the sacred
>   Fire that dances within the form of
>   every creation.

Hold your dagger over the incense, saying:

> Great God Freyr, bless this creature of
>   Air to your service.
> May we always listen to the spirit winds
>   that bring us the voices of the Ancient
>   Ones.

Put a little incense on the charcoal and, using
the chains, briefly touch the burner to the pentacle, then raise the burner high, saying:

Great Freyr, be you adored!

Carry the burner around the circle clockwise, beginning in the east. Return it to the altar.

Light the yellow candle in the east and say:

I call upon you, Powers of Air, to witness this rite and to guard this circle.

Light the red candle in the south and say:

I call upon you, Powers of Fire, to witness this rite and to guard this circle.

Light the blue candle in the west and say:

I call upon you, Powers of Water, to witness this rite and to guard this circle.

Finally, light the green candle in the north and say:

I call upon you, Powers of Earth, to witness this rite and to guard this circle.

Move back to the altar, face north and raise your arms in greeting:

This circle is bound,
With power all around.
Within it I stand
With protection at hand.

Light the three candles around the cauldron. Say:

I call upon the blessed Lady, queen of the harvest, giver of life and of plenty since before time began. Give to me, as of old, your joy and beauty, power and prosperity.

Salute the ivy-filled cauldron with your dagger or sword. Say:

> I call upon the Lord of the harvest, sacred King, giver of riches and of protection since before time began. Give to me, as of old, your strength and laughter, power and prosperity.

Take the ribbon-tied dagger in your power hand, the wine chalice in the other. Say:

> Always has life fulfilled its cycle and led to life anew in the eternal chain of the living. In honor of the Asa-Gods and their blessings, I mark the fullness of my life and the harvest of this year's lessons.

Walk three times clockwise around the circle, chanting:

> The year wheel turns and bounty comes.

Move back to the altar and lay aside the dagger. Set the wine chalice briefly on the pentacle. As you make the following toasts, each time raise the chalice high before taking a sip:

> To the good seasons that have gone and the good ones yet to come. Blessed be!
>
> To the beauty of autumn and good friends. Blessed be!
>
> To the God! May he protect this follower and bring me prosperity and happiness! Blessed be!

*To the Goddess! May she bring peace
and fulfillment to all her children!
Merry meet and merry part and merry
meet again. Blessed be!*

Now is a time for divination, meditation, or spellwork. If any spellworking is done, finish with:

*By the powers of the ancient Gods,
I bind all power within this circle
Into this spell. So mote it be!*

Extinguish the eastern candle and say:

*Depart in peace, O Powers of Air.
My thanks and blessings.*

Extinguish the southern candle and say:

*Depart in peace, O Powers of Fire.
My thanks and blessings.*

Extinguish the western candle and say:

*Depart in peace, O Powers of Water.
My thanks and blessings.*

Finally, extinguish the northern candle and say:

*Depart in peace, O Powers of Earth.
My thanks and blessings.*

Return to the altar, raise your arms and say:

*To all beings and powers of the visible
and invisible, depart in peace.
May there always be harmony between
us.*

My thanks and blessings.

Cut the circle to end the ritual. Say:

The circle is open, yet ever it remains a circle.
Around and through me always flows its magical power.

Be sure to put out your offering for the nature spirits.

Feast of Fallen Warriors

(November—Veterans' Day or The Feast of the Einherar)

Special Notes: A time to honor all fallen warriors. A special ritual to acknowledge Odhinn who welcomes all warriors, and Freyja as the Queen of the Valkyries. A sacrificial feast of cookies or cakes in animal and human shapes is appropriate.

Altar Supplies: burner, incense, chalice of water, salt, pentacle, chalice of wine, dagger and sword, 4 Element candles, plate of bread and salt, apple, cauldron, cookies. White candle in cauldron with red candle on the left, black on the right.

Cast the circle with the dagger or sword, saying:

> I consecrate this circle of power to the
>   Ancient Gods.
> Here may they manifest and bless their
>   child.

Go back to the altar, facing north, and raise your hand or wand in greeting. Say:

> This is a time that is not a time, in a
>   place that is not a place, on a day that
>   is not a day.
> I stand at the threshold between the
>   worlds, before the Gates of Asgard.
> May the Ancient Ones help and protect
>   me on my magical journey.

Set the chalice of water on the pentacle. Hold your dagger over the chalice, saying:

> *Great Goddess Freyja, bless this crea-*
> *ture of Water to your service.*
> *May we always remember the cauldron*
> *waters of rebirth.*

Hold your dagger over the salt, saying:

> *Great Goddess Freyja, bless this crea-*
> *ture of Earth to your service.*
> *May we always honor the blessed Earth,*
> *its many forms and beings.*

Sprinkle a little salt into the water, then hold the chalice up high. Say:

> *Great Freyja, be you adored!*

Sprinkle the water mixture lightly around the edges of the circle, moving clockwise and beginning in the east. Replace the chalice on the altar. Hold your dagger over the incense burner, saying:

> *Great God Freyr, bless this creature of*
> *Fire to your service.*
> *May we always remember the sacred*
> *Fire that dances within the form of*
> *every creation.*

Hold your dagger over the incense, saying:

> *Great God Freyr, bless this creature of*
> *Air to your service.*
> *May we always listen to the spirit winds*
> *that bring us the voices of the Ancient*
> *Ones.*

Put a little incense on the charcoal and, using the chains, briefly touch the burner to the pentacle, then raise the burner high, saying:

Great Freyr, be you adored!

Carry the burner around the circle clockwise, beginning in the east. Return it to the altar.

Light the yellow candle in the east and say:

I call upon you, Powers of Air, to witness this rite and to guard this circle.

Light the red candle in the south and say:

I call upon you, Powers of Fire, to witness this rite and to guard this circle.

Light the blue candle in the west and say:

I call upon you, Powers of Water, to witness this rite and to guard this circle.

Finally, light the green candle in the north and say:

I call upon you, Powers of Earth, to witness this rite and to guard this circle.

Move back to the altar, face north and raise your arms in greeting:

This circle is bound,
With power all around
Within it I stand
With protection at hand.

Light the black candle to the right of the cauldron. Salute the altar with your sword. Say:

This is the time to honor all fallen warriors. Great Odhinn, All father, you who have gathered to you all brave war-

riors who die in battle, I salute you.

Light the red candle to the left of the cauldron. Salute the altar with your sword. Say:

Freyja, Queen of the Valkyries, you who have gathered to you your share of the fallen heroes, I salute you.

Light the white candle in the cauldron. Salute the altar again with the sword. Say:

Hail to the fallen warriors who now dwell in Asgard. I salute your courage, your willingness to die in defense of your family, your property, your community, your country. Well do I know that brave warriors do not all fall in wars. They sacrifice themselves as policemen on the streets. They greet the Valkyries when rescuing others in peril. They meet the Allfather as firemen on duty. The fallen warriors of Asgard have walked all paths of life, yet because of their deeds were found worthy by the Valkyries, warrior-women who see the truth in the heart of each person.

Lay sword before altar. Take up dagger and apple:

As there is death in life, so must there be life in death. The symbol of the Lady and life eternal is hidden inside the sacred fruit of Idhunn, the Maiden. Only those who seek and know may find it.

Cut the apple crosswise to reveal the pentagram made by the core and seeds:

> *Behold! The star of Life! Symbol of the Triple Goddess who, with the Allfather, brings forth new beginnings out of the cauldron of rebirth.*

Eat part of the apple, saving the rest to be placed outside:

> *The secret of this sacred fruit is forbidden only to those who walk in darkness, those who turn away from the great knowledge that life never ends. Like a dried autumn seed, each passing soul falls into the sacred cauldron, to rest, then be reborn in another time and place.*

Place the plate of bread and salt on the pentagram for a moment. Say:

> *Behold, the staples of life! The grain which is ground and baked into bread to sustain the body. Salt which preserves food and enriches life. Each time I taste salt and bread may I remember that all life turns in cycles of life and death.*

Dip a piece of bread into the salt and eat it. Place the plate of cookies on the pentagram. Go the east. Salute with the sword, say:

> *Rulers of Air, give your blessings to the fallen warriors. Grant them rest in spring fields caressed by gentle breezes.*

Go the south. Salute with the sword, say:

> *Rulers of Fire, give your blessings to*

the fallen warriors. Grant them sunny
days and warm nights of feasting.

Go to the west. Salute with the sword, say:

Rulers of Water, give your blessings
to the fallen warriors. Grant them warm
pools of refreshing water where they
may dream of rebirth.

Go to the north. Salute with the sword, say:

Rulers of Earth, give your blessings to
the fallen warriors. Grant them changing seasons, green forests, and sweet
meadow flowers.

Return to the altar. Salute with the sword,
say:

Great Odhinn, you who see beyond all
actions to the truth, carry my greetings
and blessings to the heroes of Asgard.
Although we may grieve their loss
among us, yet do we rejoice that they rest
with you. Let them know they are not forgotten.

Place the wine chalice on the pentacle for a
few moments, then lift it high, saying:

To the Gods of Asgard! Merry meet and
merry part and merry meet again.

Drink the wine, saving some back to be put
outside for the nature spirits.

Now is a time for divination, meditation, or
spellwork. If any spellworking is done, finish
with:

By the powers of the ancient Gods,
I bind all power within this circle
Into this spell. So mote it be!

Extinguish the eastern candle and say:

Depart in peace, O Powers of Air.
My thanks and blessings.

Extinguish the southern candle and say:

Depart in peace, O Powers of Fire.
My thanks and blessings.

Extinguish the western candle and say:

Depart in peace, O Powers of Water.
My thanks and blessings.

Finally, extinguish the northern candle and say:

Depart in peace, O Powers of Earth.
My thanks and blessings.

Return to the altar, raise your arms and say:

To all beings and powers of the visible
and invisible, depart in peace.
May there always be harmony between
us.
My thanks and blessings.

Cut the circle to end the ritual. Say:

The circle is open, yet ever it remains a
circle.
Around and through me always flows
its magical power.

Be sure to put out your offering for the nature

spirits. Tie the cookies and pieces of the apple to tree limbs for the birds and animals.

8. Introduction to the Norse and Vikings

History

The Teutonic tribes came to settle in the Scandinavian peninsula, on islands of the Baltic Sea, and in northern Germany about three or four centuries before the Christian era. They were of Indo-European stock with the same basic language, customs and beliefs. They later became the Viking raiders who terrorized and settled parts of Europe, Britain, Scotland, Ireland, Greenland and Iceland.

In their own language, a *vikingr* was a raider; the phrase *fara i viking* meant to go raiding over the seas. A typical Northman was tall and blonde with blue or grey eyes. However, there were "black" Vikings—not black of skin, but with dark hair and eyes.

The Vikings carried their cult of Thorr to every land they settled. In fact, the Irish called the Vikings of Dublin "the tribe of Thorr."

Like the Celts, the Norse had skalds (bards)

who memorized their genealogies, legends and history. None of this was written down until much later in Icelandic chronicles.

The skalds were skilled poets, whose responsibility it was to remember correctly the family genealogies, myths and epics. Unlike the Celtic bards, they could not scorn a king in song, but could use their skills to break bad news, give advice, buy life, or mock death. Skaldic poetry was long and full of kennings, vivid descriptions and history. These poets held Odhinn in high regard and called poetry "sacred mead."

A kenning was a phrase which all hearers knew was an image of something else. "Fire of Odin" and "fire of the Valkyries" often were used to depict a sword; "hawksfell," a hand; "falcon's tree," a human forearm; "ship of the Dwarves," poetry; "tears of Freyja" or "cushion of the dragon Fafnir" gold; "reddening of spears" or "the Valkyries' magic song," battle; "wound-dew," blood; "to feed the ravens" or "to sate the eagles," killing enemies.

Although from very early times the Norse were divided into three classes, Thrall (slave), Karl (farmer), and Jarl (chieftain or aristocrat), there was no pure warrior class. Every man had to be a fighter. Even women were trained to handle weapons for defense. Heimdall in the disguise of Rigr brought these classes of men into being, thus being the genetic link between the Gods and humans.

The Norsemen were Vikings perhaps in part because their countries had extremely short growing seasons, very poor rocky soil, and long

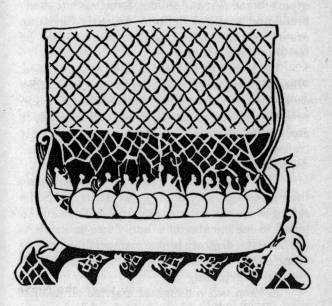

winters. It was a hard life that shaped men to be daring, adventurous and aggressive. Their ships and weapons were the finest in Europe. They were expert horsemen and sailors, ferocious but sometimes undisciplined fighters. An early Christian prayer lists the phrase: Lord, deliver us from the terror of the Northmen!

Luck ranked highest in desirable qualities. When fighting men prepared to go viking, they chose a leader known for his battle-luck. Christian priests were known for their lack of weather-luck among the Norse. No ship's captain willingly transported one. If he had to, and a storm arose, the priest was immediately thrown overboard.

The Vikings took great pride in knowing their genealogies for many generations and had a strong sense of what was due from a kinsman. An insult to one member of a family was an insult to all; likewise, disgrace by one member affected everyone else. Both men and women were independent and enterprising.

Seldom was a daughter married off against her will. Weddings were formalized before witnesses by the bride and groom drinking the bridal ale. Divorces were simple—a declaration before witnesses at the Assembly (Thing) on the grounds for parting and a return of the dowry. No stigma was involved.

The Norse believed strongly in their code of honor and freedom. They were outspoken, fearless in battle, and steadfast in friendship, even to the taking of sworn blood-bonds. A man, fostered to another family early in childhood could claim the same rights and help from his foster family as from kin.

On occasion, the Thing (court of law) would pass sentence, fine or outlaw an uncontrollable man. They had a detailed, strict code of repayment, or weregild, for the death or injury of any human or domestic animal. Since the Norse considered their good name of prime importance, gossip was regarded as one of the worst crimes possible. Offense taken at slurs to honor led to many blood-feuds that lasted for generations.

Conversion to Christianity nearly wiped out the Teutonic mythological epics. But Scandinavia and Iceland managed to preserve the sagas and epics, leaving us a rich assortment of history and belief. Pictorial symbols of their legends and deities can still be seen, cleverly carved in Christian churches.

Religion

Most sites for worship were in the open air in holy groves and meadows, before holy wells, special rocks, trees or hillocks. But there were also wooden temples, probably built much like the Norse long houses, and marked off by fences built in a V-shape barrier. Inside these areas no blood could be shed or weapons carried. Sometimes wooden posts with human faces depicted the deities. The temples and even outdoor shrines were laid out on a north-south axis, and the people faced north to pray. In contrast to records from the Roman Age, references to human sacrifice in the Vi-

king Age are rare.

The landvaettir were powerful land-spirits who lived in the Earth and were responsible for it. Offerings were placed for them at cairns, caves and hillocks. The terrible dragon-heads on the Viking ships were removed before land was sighted so that the landvaettir would not be frightened away.

Yarrow and mistletoe were among the herbs used for ceremonies. Lurs (long twisting horns) were used solely for religious purposes, but harps, bells and drums were used for both religious rites and personal entertainment.

There were full-time priests and priestesses in the temples. Among the people were men and women who practiced as seers, looking into the future and doing various magical rites. A *vitki* was a magician or wise one.

There is evidence to indicate that the terrifying berserkers were initiates of an Odhinn cult. It was believed that they could change themselves into animals whenever they wished. They did leaping dances with spears and swords and wearing horned helmets. These men were usually part of a chieftain's household, not marrying until they retired. To induce their battle frenzies, they may have used a type of self-hypnosis or trance-inducing plants. It was well known that neither fire nor steel could stop them in battle; only an instant death-wound could bring down a berserker.

The god Thorr was called the common man's friend. Offerings of meat and bread were laid out in his temples. In these buildings a huge sacred arm-ring on which oaths were taken and heavy bronze hammers were also kept. His symbol, the double-bladed axe or hammer, was used to bless births, marriages, deaths and cremations. The hammer was considered such a protection against all evil that men and women wore tiny hammer amulets. Fighting men worshipped Thorr as the strongest god and Tyr for magical influences in battle.

Freyr, as the god of fertility, was also called upon to bless marriages. Bells and hand clapping were performed in his rituals. Sacred horses were kept in some of his sanctuaries. In the *Vatnsdaela Saga,* there is mention of such a horse, a stallion called Freyfaxi (mane of Freyr).

Odhinn was not much trusted by the average Viking, although he was the chief God of Asgard and was worshipped by chieftains, skalds and berserkers. Odhinn's main purpose was to fend off the terrible destiny he knew awaited the Gods and humans at Ragnarök. This put him and his actions above the human concept of good and evil.

A sacred symbol of both Freyr and Freyja was the boar. Boar images were used on ceremonial objects and war helmets. Some Teutonic tribes wore masks or helmets that covered the face and had a tusk protruding on each side. A Swedish king had a helmet Hildigoltr (battle pig) and won another helmet called Hildisvin (battle swine). Neck-rings and arm-rings also carried the boar symbol.

Wise women, seeresses, rune-mistresses and healers were closely connected with Freyja, goddess of magic and love affairs (not marriages). The female *völva* went about the tribes giving predictions of the future through trance and were linked to cults of both Freyja and Odhinn. They also did healing and occasionally cursing. They did not tend to marry, although they did take lovers. These women carried a staff with a bronze cap or mounting and wore capes, hoods and gloves of fur.

Seidr was a form of magic, trance and divination that originated with Freyja and was a feminine mystical craft. It was fairly independent of runic magic, being more involved with shape-shifting, astral body travel through the nine worlds, sex magic and other techniques.

Freyja was also known as the great *dis*. The *disir* (goddesses) were nine women dressed in black and carrying swords. Nine (a Moon number) was considered the most sacred and mysterious of numbers. At the beginning of winter, particularly in Sweden, these "spirits" and Freyja were worshipped in a ceremony called the *disablot*. The *disir* brought good luck but they were also merciless in exacting justice.

Smithcraft was a mystical art as it included not only metalworking, but woodcarving, carpentry, bone carving and other forms of handicraft. A smith had to be knowledgeable about runes as it was his responsibility to engrave the correct ones on sword hilts.

Three important symbols used in early Scandinavian rock carvings were ships, horses and the Sun-wheel. Ships were often connected with death and burial. Dead warriors were sometimes buried in mounds shaped like ships. There is also evidence that some were laid out in ships which were then set afire and sometimes launched on the sea.

In Germany, the dragon was guardian of the

burial mound. German dragons had wings and a long tail, while Norse dragons were shaped like serpents. Jormungand, World-Serpent, who inhabited the Ocean surrounding Earth, was depicted as a long, slender, wingless dragon.

In Norse mythology, Asgard (Heaven) was the realm of the gods where those who died violently, warriors, and righteous men went after death. There is nothing to suggest that women did not have the same privileges. Helheim, the kingdom of the goddess Hel, had one section for criminals, another for those who died of old age or illness. Oath-breakers and secret killers, two unforgivable crimes to the Norse, were also condemned to Hel's kingdom.

Predestination and predetermination were unknown to the Norse. They believed, however, that what each person did influenced his or her future. This idea is reflected in their descriptions of the Norns. Urd was defined as "that which has become," Verthandi as "that which is becoming," and Skuld as "that which should become." The Vikings also believed in an afterlife and continuing contact between the living and the dead.

The Norse religious rituals encompassed the solstices and equinoxes, but primarily they were used for everyday happenings, such as plowing, harvest, birth, marriage, death, traveling, trade undertakings, etc. In other words, they approached the gods whenever they felt a need. The most powerful times for rituals were thought to be dawn, noon, evening and midnight.

An example of a personal ritual was the naming of a child. Not until it was certain that a newborn child would live was it sprinkled with water and given a name.

The runes were both magical symbols and letters of the alphabet, which had few curved lines. Many leading Northmen learned them as part of their education. They believed that knowledge of the runes could save a man's life, blunt sword blades, calm the seas and winds, quench fire, and help to understand the language of birds.

A *rynstr* or runester was very skilled in the knowledge of the runes. He had to know how the runes should be carved, how they should be read, how they should be colored and how they should be used. In ancient German, the word "to make red" and "to endow with magical power" were the same.

Dress and Ornamentation

Everyday clothing was simple among the Norse. Men wore long-sleeved wool shirts and trousers with attached socks. Tall leather boots and sleeveless jerkins completed the outfit. Mustaches were common; hair was cut below the ear, except for warriors who wore it long and braided or fastened in an elaborate top knot. Their trousers were either very full or very straight and tight in the legs. Nearly every man carried a dagger and sword on his leather belt.

Warriors wore a chain mail shirt over a padded leather jerkin and usually a conical metal helmet with nose and cheek pieces. Helmets with wings and horns were rare among fighting men. These types of helmets were mainly used for religious ceremonies. A warrior carried a round, wooden, leather-covered shield and a long, broad, two-edged sword. Across his back were hung leaf-bladed spears, "the serpent of battle." The favorite Viking weapon, however, was the battle-axe with its large curved blade and four-foot handle. It could cleave completely through a helmet and skull.

Swords were made in such a way as to be strong and flexible, seldom shattering against helmet or shield rim. They were beautiful, highly prized possessions, passed down from father to son, and given names, like "Leg-Biter." Battle-axes and shields had names also, usually pertaining to Trolls, blood and death.

Women wore long plain wool dresses over linen petticoats for everyday. Wool socks and soft leather shoes covered their feet. A great brooch at one shoulder held a collection of necessary tools on little chains: scissors, keys, needle and thread case, etc. A dagger hung from the belt. Their hair was long, either hanging down or piled up in elaborate styles.

In cold weather both sexes wore thick heavy cloaks and fur hats. Ornaments of all kinds—rings, earrings, brooches, torcs, bracelets, collars, arm-rings, neck-rings, pins, necklaces, diadems—were much favored. This jewelry was worked into shapes of animals, leaves, vines, or flowers. "The fire," as Vikings called gold, was a desired metal, but copper, silver and bronze were also used. Amber amulets were worn for luck.

The Norse were mainly monogamous; only kings and great chiefs had concubines. Illegitimate children were treated generously, often adopted by the father and given the same training as his other children.

These people built long houses, 40-100 feet in length, made of logs or planks and roofed with thatch or shingles. There was a door at each end, no windows, and long platforms along each inside wall. Two rows of wooden pillars helped to hold up the roof. A fire pit lay in the center of the pounded earth floor.

All types of wild game, beef, pork, chicken and mutton were eaten along with a variety of vegetables, fruits and breads. Milk drinks, weak barley beer and mead rounded out the meals. Mead, made of fermented honey and water, was drunk from tankards or drinking horns. Knives and spoons were known, but not forks.

9. Myths and Deities

In Norse mythology, life began without any one creator. In the beginning there was a magic-filled gulf (Ginnungagap) bounded on the north by cold and darkness (Niflheim) and on the south by fire (Muspell). Life began at the place where the positive energy of Muspell melted the negative energy of Niflheim. These flashing sparks of life and hailstones of cold combined to produce the life-seeds of all matter.

From the Sun's warmth on the whirling life-seeds came Audhumla, the great cow, and Ymir, a Giant. Audhumla licked a being, Buri, out of the salty ice. Both Ymir and Buri were asexual beings, capable of spawning offspring without a mate. Ymir perspired in his sleep, producing his Giant children. Buri produced a male being called Borr. Borr married Bestla, one of Ymir's Giantess daughters; their children were Odhinn, Vili and Ve. These offspring created the first human man (Askr or ash) and woman (Embla or elm) out of living trees by giving them a new form, intelligence and a soul.

But Ymir was terribly cruel, so Odhinn and his brothers killed him. The whole race of Giants drowned in Ymir's blood, except for Bergelmir (Mountain Old) and his wife who hid in the great World-Mill. From this pair came all the Jotnar, or Giants.

The great World-Mill was used to grind the mold that made earth. Odhinn and his brothers put Ymir's body in the millstones. From his flesh they made earth, from his bones the rocks and mountains. His jaw and teeth became boulders, his blood the rivers and seas. His brain and skull were set in place to make the sky. The bodies of the other Giants were also ground up to make sand and pebbles.

Maggot-like creatures crawling from Ymir's flesh were changed by Odhinn into Dwarves, small human-shaped creatures. However, he left them the color of the Earth in which they live. Their king is Modsognir. There are three tribes of Dwarves: one lives in mounds of earth, another in rocks, and the third in the high mountains. Four of the Dwarves were given the permanent task of holding up the sky. They were named for the four directions: Nordhri (North), Austri (East), Sudhri (South), and Vestri (West).

Odhinn set the heavens swinging around Veraldar Nagli (World Spike) which is the North Star, also known as Odhinn's Eye. He hung bright sparks of fire from Muspell inside Ymir's skull as stars. The Sun and Moon, larger fire-sparks, were carried across the heavens in chariots made by the Elf-smith sons of Ivaldi. Children of the vanquished Mundilferi, a rival of Odhinn's, were appointed to drive the chariots.

Mundilferi's daughter Sol drives the Sun chariot with the horses Arvakr (Early Dawn) and Alsvid (Scorching Heat). Her brother Mani drives the Moon chariot. With him are two kidnapped children—a boy Hjuki and a girl Bil. Bil was petitioned by the skalds to sprinkle magic song-mead on them from the Moon. The Milky Way was known as Bil's Way, named after this girl who rides in the Moon chariot with Mani.

The chariots of the Sun and Moon are eternally chased by two evil wolves, Giants in disguise. Skoll (Adherer) chases the Sun; Hati (Hater) chases the Moon. At Ragnarök the wolves will catch and eat the celestial bodies.

Nott or Nat (Night) is the dark daughter of Mimir, or Narfi (the Binder). She brings inspiration, peace and rest to humankind. Her second husband was Annar (Water) by whom she had the Giantess Jord, who became the mother of Thorr by Odhinn. Her third husband is Delling, red Elf of dawn; their son is Dag or Dagr (Day).

Ivaldi is the watchman of the Spring of Hvergelmir and the rivers Elivagar in Hel. His first wife was Sol, the Sun goddess. The daughters from this union were Idhunn, wife of Bragi, and the swan maidens of the western realm of Njord. His second wife was the Giantess Greip, the mother of Thjatsi-Volund, Orvandel-Egill (the great archer), and Ide. Egill's son Svipdag will destroy Thorr's hammer with the "Sword of Victory" in the last days.

The Spring of Hvergelmir (Roaring Cauldron) is the source of all water and rises up through the treeYggdrasil to all the worlds. It lies in the lowest level of the nine worlds and has one of Yggdrasill's roots deep within it.

Yggdrasil as a cosmic tree is sometimes called an ash and sometimes a yew. A clue to the correct name may be in another Norse word for yew which is needle ash. Yggdrasil, otherwise known as the World Tree, grows out of the past, lives in the present and reaches toward the future. It nourishes all spiritual and physical life. Its roots reach into all the worlds; its boughs hang above Asgard.

Yggdrasil has three main roots which hold everything together. One root reaches into the Well of Urd in Asgard, another into the Fountain of Mimir in Midgard, and the third into the Spring of Hvergelmir in Hel. At Hvergelmir is the watchman Ivaldi and his sons who defend Hel against the Storm Giants.

The World Tree is constantly under attack by evil creatures. In Niflheim, the dragon Nidhogg continually chews on its root. In Midgard, four giant harts eat the buds and leaves. Age rots its sides, and many serpents of the dark underworld attack its wood. But the Norns sprinkle it each morning with water from Urd's fountain of life.

Of the nine worlds in Norse mythology, Asgard is on the highest level, with Alfheim to the east and Vanaheim to the West. The *Prose Edda* states that Midgard is in the center of Ginnun- gagap, an area of 11 rivers and frozen wasteland. It is Midgard that ties together all the other worlds. On the same level as Midgard is Svar- talfheim to the south, Nidavellir to the east, and Jotunheim to the west. Below Midgard lie Hel and Niflheim.

The Aesir gods live in Asgard, the Vanir in Vanaheim, and the Light Elves in Alfheim or Ljos- salfheim (Light Elf-World).

In the sky between Asgard and Midgard hangs the beautiful Bifrost bridge, guarded by the god Heimdall. Heimdall wears silver armor and a helmet with ram's horns. From his tower Himinbjorg (Ward of Heaven), which sits on the highest point of Bifrost, he guards the bridge. He can see a hundred leagues by day or night, can hear grass growing, and sleeps very little. He is also called Gullintani (Golden Teeth).

The southern span of Bifrost reaches to Midgard. The bridge is built of air and water with protecting fire on its edges. Everyday the Gods ride their horses and chariots across the bridge to the lower world Thingstead. Thorr, however, has to walk as his thunder chariot could destroy Bifrost.

Asgard is situated on an island in the middle of a broad dark river which flows up through Yg- gdrasil from Hvergelmir. Around Asgard is a high wall (the story of its construction is given later). The flames of the boiling river lap the base

Yggdrasil, from Finn Magnusen's EDDALAEREN, *Copenhagen, 1824.*

of the wall, thus making Asgard impossible to enter except through Odhinn's mighty gate.

In the middle of Asgard is Valaskjalf, the Court of Judgment or High Thingstead of the Gods. Here they discuss and decide their private affairs. This great hall is roofed with silver and all the walls are overlaid with burnished gold. Odhinn's great throne is here, with twelve golden seats around it for the other gods who sit in judgment with him.

Vingolf (Abode of Friends) is the beautiful sanctuary, as well as private Thingstead, for the Goddesses in Asgard.

Also in Asgard is a smithy where the Elf-smiths, or Dwarves, such as Ivaldi's sons and Sindri's kinsmen, work in fine metals, making all kinds of implements and objects for the Gods.

Freyr, the brother of the goddess Freyja, was the ruler of the Light Elves in his youth. A very interesting group of Elves were the sons of Ivaldi—Volund (Weland) and his brothers. They had many traits of Dwarves, Giants and star deities, and were symbolized as mountain wolves and often winged. In Teutonic myths, Elf-smiths were stronger than Giants.

On the middle level are Midgard (Earth or manifested material world of men), Jotunheim (Land of the Giants or Etins), Nidavellir (Land of the Dwarves) and Svartalfheim (Land of the Dark Elves). Midgard is surrounded by a deep Ocean; in it lives the monster World-Serpent. Another name for Midgard is Mannaheim (home of men).

In Jotunheim, which occupies the east edge

of the world of men, lies the mountain stronghold (Utgard) of the Giants. Mountain Giants are bound to their mountains. Their mothers, often called Hags, are greater than the males. Not all of them are against the Gods. The Hag Grid warned and instructed Thorr.

Niflheim is the world of the dead, ruled by the goddess Hel, while the kingdom Hel is the realm of the dead, ruled by Urd. Muspell is guarded by the Fire Giant Surt and his flaming sword.

Niflheim or Niflhel (Misty Hel or Misty World) lies to the south of Midgard. It is an immense land of darkness and great cold, an area of torture for evil souls.

To reach Niflheim, one has to travel downwards for nine days from Midgard on the Helway. This road goes through great forests and deep dark valleys, over high mountains. There is a deep black cave between the two levels of Midgard and Hel. Near the end of the Helway, the maiden Modgud guards the Gjallarbru or Gjoll (Howling) bridge over the boundary river Gjoll. Beyond the bridge are the Hel Gates (Helgrind), and behind them the Hall of Death. The goddess Hel's palace is called Sleetcold or Sleet-Den.

Dwarves and Dark Elves live in mines, tunnels, caves and holes in Nidavellir and Svartalfheim, respectively, located below Midgard and above Hel. It is believed by some that Dwarves and Dark Elves are the same creatures.

Hel is the lower world Thingstead of the Gods. There the souls of the dead are judged by Odhinn, and rewards or punishments handed out. Even the Valkyries must first bring their chosen warriors to this Thingstead where they are accepted or rejected as unworthy.

At the lower world Thingstead, the Hamingjur (individual guardian spirits, personal power, or the luck of each man) can speak for an individual during judgment. If the person is evil, he or she is deserted by his or her Hamingja. Those souls judged good go to Hel where they live in eternal joy. Those condemned as evil are shackled and driven to Niflhel by the Dark Elves. There they must drink burning venom and are subjected to the nine realms of torture.

Two races of deities ended up in Asgard, the Aesir and the Vanir. The Vanir-goddess Gullveig (Gold-Thirst) went to the Aesir and flaunted her ability to predict the future and make gold. When she refused to share her secrets with them, the Aesir killed and burned her. This proved ineffective; twice Gullveig rose from the flames. Finally the Aesir gave up. They renamed her Heid (Gleaming One) and began to consider a peaceful life with the Vanir more seriously.

However, the murder attempt brought about constant fighting, with neither side getting the upper hand. The walls of both kingdoms were destroyed. Finally a truce was called, and hostages exchanged. The greatest Vanir deities, Njord, Freyr and his sister Freyja (supreme Goddess of magic), joined the Aesir.

Meanwhile, the Vanir were having their own problems with the two Aesir hostages, Mimir and Hoenir. Mimir was very wise, but Hoenir was mostly silent. When he did speak, it was evident that he was not very bright. In disgust, the Vanir took out their frustrations on Mimir, relieving him of his head which they sent back to Odhinn. The Allfather preserved it with herbs and placed it at the Fountain in Midgard, so that Mimir's knowledge would not be lost.

When Mimir was slain, his seven sons fell asleep in their hall in Hel. When Heimdall blows his horn at Ragnarök, Mimir's sons will awake and fight with the Gods of Asgard against their enemies.

Odhinn's knowledge stems from several sources. According to the *Ynglinga Saga* he learned the magical art called *seid* from Freyja; but still he thirsted for more magical knowledge. In frustration, he hanged himself from Yggdrasill for nine days and nights. At the very last of his endurance, Odhinn saw the runes written clearly and understood them. Elsewhere we learn that he gave up one eye to drink the egg-white mead of the Fountain of Mimir, thus gaining all knowledge, and becoming worthy of ruling the Asa-Gods. Both of these incidents may be symbolic of shamanistic initiation experiences.

In Asgard and Vanaheim each deity has a magnificent hall. Odhinn, chief of the Gods, has two halls: Valhalla (Hall of the Slain) where he revels with fallen heroes and his Valkyries, and Valaskjalf (Seat of the Slain) where he can sit on his throne Hlidskjalf and see all of the nine worlds. Odhinn's ultimate purpose is to try to delay the terrible destiny awaiting both the Gods and humankind. Therefore, his actions and thoughts are beyond the normal concept of good and evil. He was made aware of this future fate when he called up a dead seeress in Hel. In the Voluspa (The Sibyl's Prophecy) this seeress tells him of an axe-age, a sword-age, and a wolf-age when brother will turn against brother. This will herald the beginning of Ragnarök.

Odhinn is a war god and magician who controls battles, judges the dead, gives inspiration with magic and the runes. Norse poets had over 150 names to describe him. Often he was pictured with an empty eyesocket and a long grey beard, wearing a cloak flecked with cloud-spots and a wide-brimmed hat.

The Valkyries are Odhinn's female warriors who collect his share of fallen warriors and carry them to Valhalla on their flying horses. These women wear armor and have names such as Shaker, Raging Warrior, and Shrieking. It is said that a man chosen to die in battle sees a Valkyrie just before the fatal blow. One tradition says there were thirteen Valkyries.

Sif and Thorr live in Bilskirnir (Lightning); Balder and Nanna in Breidablik. Freyja has her own hall Sessrumnir on Folkvang where she takes her half of the slain warriors. Njord and Aegir are the only gods to have halls near or under the sea. Njord's hall is called Noatun (Anchorage or Shipyard).

Miraculously, the truce held between the Aesir and the Vanir; the Gods got down to the business of replacing the damaged walls. It quickly became clear that they would need help if they were to protect themselves from attack by the Ice Giants. About this time a stranger rode up, offering to do the work. In payment he wanted the Sun, the Moon, and Freyja as his wife.

Loki, sworn blood-brother of Odhinn, suggested the Gods accept, with the condition that the building be done in six months without help. The stranger agreed as long as he could use his stallion Svadilfari (Hazard-Farer). It soon was evident that the walls would be finished on time. Loki found himself in a lot of trouble with the Gods.

But Loki was a shape-changer. He turned himself into a mare and lured the stallion away. The last of the walls remained unfinished. With a roar the stranger became his true self—a Rock Giant. The Gods killed him immediately. When Loki returned after a year, he brought with him a magical eight-legged horse named Sleipnir, offspring of Svadilfari and Loki as a mare. The Trickster gave him to Odhinn to regain his friendship.

One day a beautiful girl showed up at the gates of Asgard. She called herself Gulveig-Hoder but was really a Giantess in disguise. She was the wife of the Giant Gymir and was a spy bent on causing all the trouble she could. She became handmaiden to Freyja. Although Loki was already married to Sigyn, he took Gulveig-Hoder as a wife also. Naturally she was willing to aid his ambitions to be ruler of the Asa-Gods.

It wasn't long before Gulveig-Hoder lured Freyja out of Asgard where the goddess was captured by the Giant Beli (Howler), the father of Grep. He fled with her to his castle in Jotunheim where she remained a prisoner until rescued by Svipdag and Ull.

The Gods met at the High Thingstead and discovered who was responsible for Freyja's capture. Thorr went to find Gulveig-Hoder and struck her down. Three times the Gods burned her and twice she came back to life. The third time the Gods threw her ashes away, but Loki secretly swallowed her heart, thus becoming even more evil.

Loki was always creating trouble for the Gods. Against several dire warnings, he became involved with the Giantess Angrboda. From this union came three monsters: Jormungand, the World-Serpent; Hel, goddess of Helheim; and Fenrir, a huge wolf.

Fenrir became savage and unpredictable, even by the Gods' standards. They decided the animal had to be chained, but were unable to do it. They needed a special magic chain and some way to make Fenrir agree to the chaining. Freyr's servant, Skirnir, went to the Dwarves, who forged a magical ribbon-chain. Fenrir was afraid of the innocent looking bonds, so the god Tyr volunteered to put his hand in the wolf's jaws while the chain was fastened. Fenrir struggled but was caught fast. Before Tyr could remove his hand, the wolf bit it off.

Thorr, champion of the Gods against all Giants because of his size and strength, was Odhinn's son by the Giantess Jord. Thorr had a magic hammer, Mjollnir. Once when he and Loki were returning from one of their secret trips into Jotunheim, Thorr's hammer was stolen by the Giant Thrym while they slept. Loki borrowed Freyja's falcon-dress to search for it, but was caught by the Giants. He returned to Asgard with the demand that the Giants would return Mjollnir in exchange for Freyja as bride for their leader. The Gods considered this until Freyja exploded in anger. Even Odhinn fled the hall in fear. So the Gods met at the High Thingstead, the Goddesses at Vingolf. Heimdall came up with a plan of dressing Thorr in bridal attire and sending Loki with him dressed as a maid.

Thorr, clad in a bridal dress and veil, and dragging Loki with him, went to the hall of Thrym, the Frost Giant. All through the wedding feast, Loki had to keep assuring the Giants that the ravenous bride, who seemed to be eating and drinking more than her share, was only excited. When Mjollnir was laid in Thorr's lap to bless the marriage, the God threw aside the veil and killed the Giants.

Even Thorr's anger, however, did not permanently stop Loki's maliciousness and lying. Once Loki was captured by the Giant Thjatsi in the disguise of an eagle. The Giant would allow him to go free only if he delivered Idhunn to him. So Loki tricked Idhunn, keeper of the golden apples of immortality, into leaving Asgard. She was imprisoned by the Giant. Without the apples, the Gods began to grow old. Heimdall discovered Loki's part in the event, and the Gods made the troublemaker get Idhunn back.

Once again Loki borrowed Freyja's falcon-dress and went to Thjatsi's castle where he changed Idhunn into a nut so he could carry her back to Asgard. But before he fled, Loki made himself known to the Giant and dared him to catch him. Thjatsi in his eagle disguise almost caught Loki but the flames of the river around Asgard brought him down. Thorr killed him with his hammer.

Before long, Skadi, daughter of Thjatsi, showed up at the gates of Asgard, clad in her chain mail and helmet, and carrying a great spear and poisoned arrows. In an attempt to avenge her father's death, she challenged the Gods to combat. Since she was very beautiful, it was decided to try to appease her. Loki went outside the walls and danced for her with a goat in a most peculiar fashion until her anger vanished. Then Odhinn offered her a choice of any God as husband, but she could only choose while blindfolded. Skadi had already decided that she wanted Balder the Beautiful, so she managed to peek under the blindfold and spied a handsome foot. She chose its owner, only to discover that the foot belonged to the fair Njord, summer sea-god who stills the tempests of Aegir and the blasts of Gymir (Storm Giant of the east). The couple went to live at Noatun. However it wasn't long before Skadi missed the snow-covered mountains and thundering waterfalls of her homeland. Neither Skadi nor Njord could bring themselves to live in the other's land, and they soon parted.

An incident occurred, while Thorr was gone, in which Loki sneaked into Sif's bedroom and cut off all her golden hair with a sharp sword. Sif's hair represented harvest, corn, abundance and prosperity. With Thorr's threats ringing in his ears, Loki went to the sons of Ivaldi who made magic hair for Sif, a spear Gungnir, and the ship Skidbladnir. Some translations call these craftsmen Elves and others Dwarves. On his way home, Loki met two other craftsmen, Brokk and Eitri, who were kinsmen of Sindri, a second family of Elfsmiths. Loki bet his head against their ability to make equal or better gifts.

Brokk and Eitri forged Odhinn's arm-ring Draupnir, Thorr's hammer Mjollnir, and Freyr's boar Gullinbursti. The Gods decided the gifts were as good as the first ones, and Brokk demanded Loki's head. Clever Loki agreed, but said Brokk could have none of his neck. Brokk settled for sewing Loki's mouth shut. The other Gods' laughter at his pain made Loki decide to plot revenge.

One day Freyr sat on Odhinn's throne in the High Thingstead and from it he could see into all the nine worlds. He wasn't supposed to be on the throne, and his actions set the stage for future troubles for the Gods. While sitting on the throne, Freyr saw in the north a beautiful Giantess Gerd, daughter of Gymir. He was so overcome by love that he refused to eat or drink. Finally his servant Skirnir got Freyr to confide in him and told the other Gods what had happened. They sent Skirnir to win Gerd for Freyr. Freyr was so lovesick that he sent the Sword of Victory with his servant.

Riding on Sleipnir and bearing bridal gifts, Skirnir arrived at Gymir's castle. Gerd spurned the proposal and gifts until Skirnir threatened to send her to Niflhel forever. At last she promised to marry Freyr if the Sword of Victory was given to her father. Thus, for love of a woman, the sword that would bring disaster to the Gods passed into the Giants' hands.

Another time Loki was nosing around Jotunheim, wearing Freyja's falcon-dress, because he desired the daughter of the Giant king Geirrod. He was captured and, as usual, he won his freedom by promising to deliver Thorr to the Giants—Thorr without his magic hammer, gloves or strength belt. By much lying, Loki finally got Thorr to go with him. The sons of Ivaldi accompanied them. On the way they stopped for the night in a deep woods inhabited by a friendly Giantess Grid, mother of Odhinn's son Vidar (the Silent One). This Giantess had a magic rowan wand named Gridarvold. She warned Thorr about Loki and the Giants, and gave him her magic staff, belt and iron gloves. As a result of this gift of the rowan staff, this tree became one of Thorr's sacred plants. Thorr and his friends continued their journey through rising rivers and steep mountains to reach their destination. With the help of Grid's weapons and the arrows of Ivaldi's sons, Geirrod and his Giants were destroyed.

Balder, the summer Sun-god, was the son of

Odhinn and Frigg. On his tongue were engraved runes of eloquence. Balder began to have prophetic dreams of his death and fell into a state of melancholy. So Frigg sent her sister Fulla to all creatures, plants, metals and stones to beg protection for Balder. But the slender mistletoe was considered too weak to cause harm and wasn't asked to give a promise. These promises relieved Frigg, but Odhinn still had evil premonitions.

Riding Sleipnir, Odhinn went to Niflhel to the house Heljar-rann which belongs to Delling, red Elf of the dawn. At the east gate at the grave of a vala, Odhinn chanted magic and raised the woman's spirit. The dead vala told the Allfather that the Norns had decreed that Hodur would kill Balder.

Back in Asgard the Gods were having a good time throwing all kinds of weapons at Balder who was never harmed. In disguise, jealous Loki learned from Frigg about the mistletoe. He took a sprig of it to an Elf-smith named Hlebard. Deceiving the smith, Loki had him make the mistletoe into a deadly magic arrow. Then he went back to Asgard, where he tricked the blind god Hodur into killing Balder.

At once Hermod rode Sleipnir down into Hel to search for Balder and gain his release. The Storm Giantess, Hyrrokin, pushed Balder's funeral ship out onto the sea. Nanna, wife of Balder, died of sorrow and was burned with her husband.

In the meantime, Urd promised Hermod that if everyone wept for Balder he could return to the Gods. But Loki, in the disguise of an old Giantess named Thok (Darkness), refused to weep. Thus,

Urd would not allow Balder's return to Asgard until the time of Ragnarök.

Odhinn's son Vali, whose mother was Rind, daughter of Billing (Elf of the twilight), went seeking the blind Hodur who was hiding. He avenged Balder's death by killing Hodur. The Gods discovered that Loki had been the Giantess, but Odhinn still refused to punish him. Loki was shunned in Asgard so he stayed away, nursing his evil feelings.

At the Autumn Equinox, the Gods had a feast in Aegir's hall. Loki, uninvited, killed the guard at the door and forced his way inside. The Gods still rejected him. Loki began to taunt and ridicule them with knowledge he had acquired by sneaking around in shadows. Then he fled again into hiding. At last Odhinn saw him while sitting on his throne. Thorr and others captured the evil Loki and dragged him to the island in the gulf of Black Grief where Loki's wolf-son Fenrir was imprisoned.

There he was bound to three sharp edged rocks, and Skadi hung a poisonous snake over his head to drip burning venom on him. Sigyn, his loyal wife, sits day after day holding a dish to catch the poison. The Norse say that when Sigyn leaves to empty the dish, Loki thrashes in terrible agony, and the Earth quakes from his movements.

But Loki will have his revenge at Ragnarök (the end of the world) when he breaks free and leads the Giants against the Gods. Before Ragnarök, there will be a great winter (*fimbulvetr*) lasting three years with no summers in between. There will be constant war on Midgard; earthquakes and a great freeze will kill all of humankind, except one man and woman who will hide in Yggdrasil. The skies will darken; Jormungand will invade Midgard. The wolves Skoll and Hati will swallow the Sun and Moon. Hel, with her dead souls and the dog Garm, will burst out of Niflheim, crossing the Ocean in the boat Naglfari, which is made of dead men's nails. Hel will join with Loki, Fenrir and the Giants in war against the Gods. Heimdall's horn Gjall will sound through the nine worlds as the combatants meet on the vast plain of Vigard.

Fenrir will kill Odhinn and then will be killed by Odhinn's son Vidar. Garm and Tyr, Loki and Heimdall will destroy each other. Thorr will slay Jormungand but will die of its poison. The Earth will sink into the sea; however, Yggdrasil will survive. As new land rises, the two humans hidden in the World Tree will climb down to renew the race.

Some of the Gods will survive: Odhinn's sons Vidar and Vali, Thorr's sons Modi and Magni, Hodur and Hoenir. Balder and Nanna will return from the dead. And Thorr's hammer Mjollnir, wielded by his sons, will once again protect humans.

Supernatural Beings, Places & Things

ALFHEIM (alf-hame): Land of the Light Elves.

ANDVARI (and-varri): Dwarf; shape-shifter who lived as a pike in a pool in Svartalfheim. He was a gold-collector who cursed the gold he had to give to Loki. The cursed gold later caused Fafnir to turn himself into a dragon and brought the hero Sigurd into the story.

ANGRBODA (anger-bodda): "Distress-Bringer"; "Grief Boda"; a Giantess. She had three monster children by Loki: Fenrir, Hel, and Jormungand. Disguised as Gulveig-Hoder, she became Freyja's maid, thus becoming a spy within Asgard for the Giants.

ASGARD (ass-guard): Home of the Aesir gods.

BERGELMIR (bare-ghel-mere): A Giant; father of all Giants. He and his wife were the only two Giants to survive the flood of Ymir's blood.

BESTLA (best-lah): A Frost Giantess; daughter of Ymir; wife of Borr; mother of Odhinn, Vili and Ve.

BIFROST (bee-frost): Rainbow bridge between Asgard and Midgard; guarded by Heimdall.

BILLING: Elf of the twilight or west.

BILSKIRNIR (bill-skier-near): "Lightning"; Thorr and Sif's great hall in Asgard.

BOLVERK (boll-verk): The Giant disguise used by Odhinn to get the Mead of Poetry.

BORR (bore): A supernatural man, son of Buri and father of Odhinn.

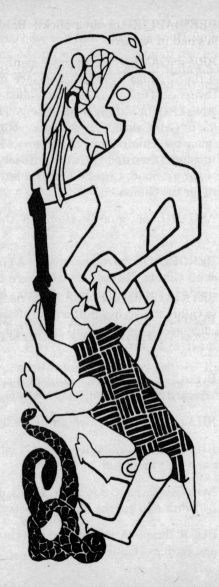

BREIDABLIK (brade-a-blick): Balder and Nanna's hall in Asgard.

BRISINGAMEN (briss-ing-a-men): "Necklace of the Brisings"; Freyja's necklace made by four Dwarves. The Brisings were called the descendants of the Shining Ones. The goddess obtained it by spending a night with each of its makers. This ornament can be worn either as a belt or a necklace depending upon how Freyja plans to use it. Brisingamen is the magical counterpart of the Midgard Serpent, and is under Freyja's control.

BROKK (brock): Dwarf; superb smith and jeweler. With Eitri he made the gold boar Gullinbursti, Odhinn's arm-ring and Thorr's hammer Mjollnir. He was pictured as small and blackened from the smithy.

BRYNHILD (brin-hild): A Valkyrie and servant to Odhinn; a shape-shifter who often used a swan disguise. This beautiful being fell in love with the hero Sigurd.

BURI (boo-ree): Supernatural being licked from the ice by Audhumla. Grandfather to the Gods.

BYGUL (bee-gool) "Bee-Gold" or honey & TRJEGUL (tree-gool) "Tree-Gold" or amber: Freyja's cats that pulled her chariot.

DARK ELVES: See Elves.

DELLING: Red Elf of the dawn or east; lover of Nott or Nat.

DISIR: Supernatural beings. See Hamingja.

DWARVES: Small human-shaped beings

created by the gods from maggots in Ymir's flesh. They live in caves and mountains in Svartalfheim; do not like daylight. They are skilled crafters, jewelers, and miners, but tend to hoard precious metals and gems. The four Dwarves sent to hold up the sky are Nordhri (North), Austri (East), Sudhri (South), and Vestri (West).

EITRI (a-tree): Dwarf and metal-worker. See Brokk.

ELVES: In Old Norse the world is *alfar*, "the shining-white one." Small human-shaped beings who have much wisdom and lore to impart. Light Elves live in Ljossalfheim or Alfheim and are helpful. Dark Elf may be another name for Dwarf. Elves live in almost every wood and stream of Midgard. Bowls of milk were left out for them.

EMBLA (em-bla): "Elm"; the first human woman created by Odhinn from a tree.

FAFNIR (fahf-near): Son of a magician/farmer, he turned into a dragon because of his greed for a hoard of gold. He was killed by his nephew Sigurd.

FARBAUTI (far-bowt-ee): "Cruel Striker"; a Fire Giant; father of Loki.

FENRIR (fen-rear) /FENRIS WOLF: Wolf-monster son of Loki; enemy of the Gods. He was so vicious that the Gods had to finally chain him.

FOUNTAIN OF MIMIR: Well in Midgard (or perhaps Jotunheim); also known as the Fountain of Knowledge.

FJALAR (fyah-lar): Dwarf and brother of

Galar; they killed Kvasir and made the Mead of Poetry from his blood.

FULLA (fool-ah): Sister of Frigg. She cares for Frigg's magic box and slippers. May have been one of the Asynjor.

GALAR (gay-lar): See Fjalar.

GARM: Monster dog who guards the island where Loki and his wolf-son are chained. Hound of the Underworld.

GERD/GERDA (gird): Frost Giantess who married Freyr. She is known for her shining beauty.

GERI (gir-ee) or Greedy & FREKI (frik-ee) or Voracious: Odhinn's great wolves.

GIANTS/GIANTESSES: Supernatural beings who are known as Frost, Fire or Mountain (Rock) Giants. All but a few are enemies of the Gods. In Old Norse the word *risi* meant a true Giant of great size, capable of intermarrying with humans; they were usually beautiful and good. The *jotnar*, singular *jotunn*, had great strength and age and were also called etins. The *thursar*, singular *thurs*, were antagonistic, destructive, and stupid. Utgard, the Giant stronghold, lies in Jotunheim. Frost Giants are extremely cold; Fire Giants hot-tempered; Mountain Giants hard as rock. All are shape-shifters and quick to do violence.

GIMLI (geem-lee): Golden-roofed hall in Asgard for righteous men after death.

GINNUNGAGAP (ghin-un-ga-gap): Great

wasteland between Niflheim and Muspell. Midgard is said to be in the center of this world

GJALL (gyall)/**GJALLARHORN**: Heimdall's mighty horn.

GJALLARBRU (gyall-ar-broo): "Resounding Bridge"; bridge crossed by Hermod on his way to Hel's realm in search of Balder.

GLADSHEIM (glahds-hame): Part of Asgard for the gods.

GNA (gnah): Servant of Frigg and a Asynjor. A messenger; her horse was called Hofvarpnir.

GRID (greed): Giantess who warned Thorr against Geirrod and Loki. She gave Thorr his magic strength belt and iron gloves.

GRIMNIR (grim-near): A disguise Odhinn used when visiting a king's court. He appeared wearing a blue cloak and large hat. The king's dogs would not bark at him.

GULLFAXI (gool-fax-ee): "Golden Mane"; horse of the Giant Hrungnir, he could gallop through the air. Thorr got him when he killed the Giant, but gave the horse to his son Magni.

GULLINBURSTI (gool-in-burst-ee): "Golden Bristles"; a boar made by the Dwarves and given to Freyr; pulls Freyr's chariot at a fantastic speed.

GULLTOP (gool-top): Heimdall's horse with a golden mane; he can fly with great speed.

GUNGNIR (goong-near): Odhinn's magic spear that always returns to his hand.

GUNNLOD (goon-lod)/GUNNLAUTH/ GUNNLOED: Giantess daughter of Suttung; she guards the Mead of Poetry in an underground-cavern.

GYMIR (guy-meer): Giant father of Gerd, Freyr's wife.

HAMINGJUR: Lifelong guardians of humans, they appear to give warnings and advice by dreams. Similar to guardian angels.

HARBARD (hahr-bard): Ferryman disguise of Odhinn.

HATI (hah-tee): Son of the Giantess of Iron Wood; a huge wolf who chases the Moon.

HEIDRUN (hide-roon): The goat which provides the mead for Valhalla and feeds on the World Tree.

HEL (hell): Realm of the Dead; also the name of the Goddess of Death.

HELGRIND: "Death Gate"; barrier between the worlds of the living and the dead.

HILDISVINI (hill-dee-sveen-ee): "Battle Pig"; sow belonging to Freyja; she travels at great speeds.

HLIDSKJALF(hlid-skyalf): Odhinn's throne in the hall Valaskjalf.

HREIDMAR (hrade-mar:): Farmer/magician and father of Fafnir.

HRUNGNIR (hroong-near): Giant who raced with Odhinn. When Thorr killed him, a piece of the

Giant's whetstone lodged in Thorr's head.

HUGGINN (hoog-in) "Thought" & MUNNIN (moon-in) "Memory": Giant ravens who bring news of the nine worlds to Odhinn.

HYMIR (him-ear): Tyr's Giant mother; she did not like the Gods. Also the name of the Giant who was with Thorr when he caught Jormungand while fishing.

HYNDLA (hinnd-la): Giantess who keeps the genealogy lists and the Memory Beer.

HYRROKIN (hirro-kin): Giantess who launched Balder's funeral boat. She rides a wolf and uses a serpent for reins.

IRON WOOD: An old dark forest in Midgard; inhabited by the mother of Hati and Skoll.

IVALDI: Also called Vidfinner and Svigdar (Champion Drinker). His family was one of two families of Elf-smiths who worked in Asgard.

JARNSAXA (yarn-sax-a): Giantess lover of Thorr and mother of his sons Magni and Modi. May have been one of the Asynjor.

JORD (joord)/JORTH: "Earth"; Giantess mother of Thorr by Odhinn.

JORMUNGAND (yore-mun-gand)/MID-GARDSORMR: World-Serpent; monster son of Loki who inhabits the Ocean surrounding Midgard.

JOTUNHEIM (yot-oon-hame): Mountain home of the Giants or Jotuns, east of Midgard or over the Ocean.

KOBOLDS (co-bolds): Small human-shaped beings who live in or near barns and stables. If treated kindly, they are friendly.

KVASIR (kvah-seer): A wise human created by the Gods. The Mead of Poetry was made from his blood.

LAUFEY (lowf-ee): "Wooded Isle"; Fire Giantess mother of Loki.

LIGHT ELVES: See Elves.

LOGI (lo-ghee): Giant who lived in Utgard.

MAGNI (mag-nee): Son of Thorr and Jarnsaxa; extremely strong at birth.

MIDGARD (mid-guard): Earth; home of humans.

MJOLLNIR (myoll-near): Thorr's magic hammer and symbol.

MODGUD (mode-good): The maiden who keeps the bridge on the road into Hel.

MODI (mode-ee): Son of Thorr and Jarnsaxa; very brave.

MUSPELL (moo-spell): Part of the lower level of nine worlds; an area of fire.

NARFI (nah-vee) & **VALI** (vah-lee): Sons of Sigyn and Loki.

NIDAVELLIR: Land of the Dwarves.

NIDHOGG (need-hoog): Dragon that guards the Spring of Hvergelmir in Niflheim.

NIFLHEIM (niffle-hame): Lowest level of the

nine worlds; a land of ice and snow.

NOATUN (noah-toon): "Shipyard"; "Anchorage"; Njord's hall by the sea.

NOTT/NAT (noot): "Night"; grandmother of Thorr. Daughter of Mimir and the sister of Urd; mother of Jord and grandmother of Thorr. Her lover is Delling, red Elf of the dawn, and their son is Dag (Day). She brings refreshment and inspiration to humans.

OCEAN: Vast stretch of water around Midgard; Jormungand dwells there.

RAGNAROK(rag-na-rock): "Twilight of the Gods"; "Doom of the Gods"; great battle that will be fought between the Gods and the Giants at the end of the world. Actually, Ragnarök will be more a transformation than total destruction.

RATATOSK (rat-ah-tosk): Squirrel who lives in Yggdrasil; runs up and down the trunk carrying insults between the dragon Nidhogg and the eagle who dwells in the top branches.

SAGA (sah-gah): "Seeress"; Giantess associated with the sign of Pisces. She has a dwelling in Asgard called Sokkvabekk (Deep Stream). One of the Asynjor.

SESSRUMNIR (sess-room-near): "Many Seats"; Freyja's hall in Asgard.

SIGURD (sig-urd)/SIGURDHR: Human lover of Brynhild; could understand the speech of birds. He killed the dragon Fafnir.

SINDRI: Elf-smith who worked in Asgard.

Brokk was his brother.

SKIDBLADNIR (skid-blad-near): Freyr's magic ship; made by Dwarves.

SKOLL (skol): Monster wolf-son of the Giantess of Iron Wood; he chases the Sun.

SKRYMIR (skree-meer): "Big Boy"; disguise used by Utgard-Loki, king of the Giants.

SLEIPNIR (slape-near): 8-legged horse of Odhinn and child of Loki; can gallop over land, sea or through the air. He is cloud-grey in color and has sacred runes engraved on his teeth.

SPRING OF HVERGELMIR (hvare-ghel-meer): Well in Niflheim guarded by the dragon Nidhogg.

SURT (sert): "Black"; Fire Giant who guards the gates of Muspell and rules the fiery beings there. He carries a flaming sword.

SUTTUNG (soo-toong): Giant who guards the Mead of Poetry.

SVADILFARI (svad-ill-far-ee): Horse who belonged to a Rock Giant; mated with Loki and produced Sleipnir.

SVARTALFHEIM (svart-alf-hame): Home of the Dark Elves.

THJATSI/THIAZI (thyah-tzee): Giant and shape-shifter; father of Skadi.

THOK/THOKK: Loki's Giantess disguise when he refused to weep for Balder.

THRUD: "Strength"; daughter of Thorr and

Sif.

THRYM (thrim): Giant who stole Mjollnir and demanded Freyja as his wife.

TOOTHGNASHER & TOOTHGRINDER: Giant goats who pull Thorr's chariot. They can be eaten and revived.

TROLLS: Huge supernatural beings with great strength; enemies of the gods, especially Thorr. Very bad-tempered.

UTGARD (oot-guard): Giants' stronghold in Jotunheim.

UTGARD-LOKI (oot-guard-low-kee): King of the Utgard Giants.

VALASKJALF (val-ah-skyalf): "Seat of the Slain"; one of Odhinn's halls in Asgard. In this hall stands the throne Hlidskjalf; from it Odhinn can see into all the nine worlds.

VALHALLA (val-hal-ah): "Hall of the Slain"; Odhinn's second hall in Asgard and home of the dead warriors. Valhalla has 640 doors, rafters of huge shining spears and tiles of golden shields.

VANAHEIM (van-ah-hame): Land of the Vanir gods; on the same level as Asgard.

VE (vay) & Vili (vill-ee): Brothers of Odhinn, they helped to kill Ymir and create the nine worlds. Vili or Villi may also be identified as Lodur or Loki. Ve could also be called Hoener.

VIDAR (vee-dar): Son of Odhinn and Grid; will avenge Odhinn by killing Fenrir at Ragnarök; and will become one of the new Gods.

VIGARD (vee-guard): Huge plain where the last battle of the Ragnarök will be fought.

VINGOLF (veen-gulf): Part of Asgard for the goddesses.

WADE: Father of Weland the smith; a Giant connected with great stones and the sea.

WELL OF URD (oord): Well in Asgard tended by the Norns.

YGGDRASIL (ig-dra-sill): World Tree; giant ash or yew tree which holds the nine worlds in place by its three roots.

The Gods & Goddesses

AEGIR (a-gear): "Alebrewer"; Vana-God of the sea; can be good or evil. He and Ran have nine daughters, or undines. Gold, prosperity, sailors, sunken treasure, brewing, control of wind and waves.

AESIR (a-seer): Warrior-gods; Keepers of the Dead; one of the races of Gods in Asgard.

ALAISIAGAE: War goddesses. See Valkyries.

ASA-GODS: The Aesir; also used to refer to the Aesir and Vanir together.

THE ASYNJOR: The Goddesses; feminine version of Aesir; also female attendants of Frigg in Vingolf. One of them, a healer, was called Eir. Others were named Fjorgyn, Frimia, Fimila, Hnossa the beautiful.

AUDHUMLA (ow-doom-la): "Nourisher"; "Rich Hornless Cow"; Mother Earth: the great cow who produced Buri and nourished the Giant Ymir. Motherhood, child-rearing, home crafts.

BALDER/BALDR/BALDUR (bal-der): "The Bright One"; Aesir Sun god; Shining God; the Bleeding God; son of Odhinn and Frigg. Sacred wells sprang up from the hoof marks of his horse. Light, advice, reconciliation, beauty, gentleness, reincarnation, wisdom, harmony, happiness.

BRAGI (brah-ghee): Son of Odhinn and Frigg; married to Idhunn. God of poetry and eloquence, he greets new arrivals to Valhalla with songs of their deeds. Wit, cunning, wisdom, music, writing, the arts; patron of skalds and minstrels.

FORSETI: Son of Balder and Nanna. Justice, good laws, arbitration, peace, fairness, good judgment.

FREYJA/FREYA (fray-ah): Syr (seer); "Lady"; Great Goddess; "She who shines over the sea"; sister of Freyr and daughter of Njord; Vana-Goddess. She was married to the god Od, perhaps identical to Odhinn, who mysteriously disappeared. She weeps tears of gold, but the tears which fall into the sea become amber. Her cats, Bygul and Trjegul, pull her chariot. She owns the necklace Brisingamen and keeps half of the slain warriors in her hall. She is the mistress of cats, leader of the Valkyries, a shape-shifter, the Sage or "sayer" who inspires all sacred poetry. Thirteen is her number and Friday her day. Love, beauty, animals, sex, cats, childbirth, fire, horses, enchantments, witchcraft, gold, wealth, trance, jewelry, wisdom, foresight, magic, luck, long life, fertility, the Moon, the sea, death, music, flowers, poetry, protection.

FREYR (fray-er)/FREY/FRO: "Lord"; Vanir Sun god; "the Lover"; son of Njord; god of Yule. He owns the boar Gullinbursti, the ship Skidbladnir, and a magic sword that moves by itself through the air. Gerda or Gerd, a Giantess, is his wife. Sensual love, fertility, growth, abundance, wealth, bravery, horses, boars, protector of ships and sailors, peace, joy, happiness, rain, beauty, weather, guarantor of oaths, groves, sunshine, plant growth, sex.

FRIG (frig)/FRIGGA/FRIJA: "Well-Beloved Spouse or Lady"; Aesir Mother Goddess; wife of Odhinn; queen of the goddesses; a shape-shifter; knower of all things. Daughter of Nott or Nat and sister of Njord; mother of Balder. Independence, childbirth, cunning, cleverness, physical love, wisdom, foresight, marriage, children, fertility, destiny, magic, enchantments.

GEFION (ghev-yon)/GEFJUN: "The Giver"; Fertility goddess; a shape-shifter. May have been one of the Asynjor. Although she is not a virgin, she is the goddess to whom virgins go at death. Magical arts, prosperity, luck, plowing, crops, land, fortunate turn of events.

GULLVEIG (gool-vague): Vana-Goddess and sorceress; "Gold-Thirst"; Mistress of Magic. Perhaps identical to Freyja. Magic, seeress, prophecy, healing.

HEID (hade): "Gleaming One". See Gullveig.

HEIMDALL (hame-dall): Asa-God of Light and the rainbow; "The White God"; guardian of Bifrost bridge. He has super sight and hearing. His horse's name is Golden Forelock. He is called "the Son of the Wave" because he was born from nine waves by Odhinn's enchantment. Nine is a magic Moon number. Guardian, beginnings and endings, morning light, seriousness, defense against evil.

HEL (hell)/HELA: Queen of the Dead and Ruler of Niflheim; her home is called Sleet-Den or Sleetcold. Dark magic, revenge.

HERMOD (hair-mod): Asa-God and son of Odhinn; rode to Niflheim to try to get Balder back. Honor, bravery.

HODUR (hod-er)/HOTH/HOTHR/BJORNO-HODER: "The blind god"; Aesir god of winter; son of Odhinn and Frigg. Passiveness. Famous archer before he became blind.

HOENIR (ho-near)/HONIR: Asa-God; a great warrior but not clever. Aggressiveness, bravery.

HOLDA/HOLDE/HOLLE/HULDA (Benign)/BERTHA/BERCHTA (White Lady): North Germanic name for Hel. "White Lady"; "Black Earth Mother"; Goddess of winter and witchcraft; the Crone aspect of the Moon; rides on the Wild Hunt. She is sometimes seen riding a goat with a pack of 24 spotted hounds (her daughters) running beside her. Wyrd, fate, karma, the arts, dark magic, revenge.

IDHUNN (id-doon)/IDUN/IDUNA: Asa-

Goddess of immortality; wife of Bragi; keeper of the golden apples. Youth, responsibility, beauty, long life.

ING: Another name for Freyr. Vana-God of Earth and fertility. The Swedish royal line called themselves Ynglings, as did the Anglo-Saxon line of Berenicia.

LOKI (lo-kee): "Father of lies"; the Trickster; Sky-Traveler; Shape-Changer; Giant who is the blood-brother of Odhinn; son of the Giant Farbauti (Cruel Smiter); married Sigyn. He is handsome, attractive, and free with the ladies. A dangerous god to invoke as one can never be certain how he will answer. Earthquakes, fire, forest fires, cunning, wit, stealth, deceit, mischief, daring, agility, trickery, thieves, revenge, destruction, lecherousness, death, lies, evil, dark magic.

MIMIR (mee-meer)/MIMR/MIMI: Very wise Aesir god; his head kept at the Fountain of Mimir after his death. Wisdom, knowledge, springs, pools, inland lakes, peace, teaching, the arts.

NANNA (nan-ah)/NANA/ANNA/IN-ANNA: Asa-Goddess; "The Moon"; Great Mother; Earth Goddess; wife of Balder. Love, gentleness.

NEHALLENNIA (nee-hal-een-ia): Goddess of plenty, seafaring, fishing, fruitfulness. Her symbol is a cornucopia.

NERTHUS (near-thus)/ERCE: Earth Mother; Fertility goddess. Peace, spring, fertility, witchcraft, wealth, groves, the sea, purification.

NJORD (nyord): Vana-God of the sea; father

of Freyr and Freyja. Lives in Noatun (Boat-Town). His Giantess wife Skadi picked him for his beautiful feet. Rules fire, winds and seas. Fishing, sailors, prosperity, success, livestock, lands, journey-luck, guarantor of oaths, wisdom, stubbornness.

THE NORNS (nornz): The Fates; the Wyrd Sisters; three women usually found near the World Tree at the Well of Urd in Asgard. URD/URTH/WYRD/ERTHA/WURD/WEIRD: past, destiny. VERTHANDI/VERDNADI: present. SKULD: the future.

OD: The mysterious husband of Freyja for whom she mourned with tears of gold. Perhaps another form of the name Odhinn. No reason is ever given for his disappearance.

ODHINN(oh-din)/ODIN/WODAN/WODEN/OTHINN: Aesir King of the gods; "All-father"; Sky God; Great Father; All-Seeing; "frenzied, mad"; god of the hanged and the Wild Hunt; god of storm, rain and harvest. A shape-shifter, he makes men mad or possessed with a blind raging fury. He produces the battle panic called "battle-fetter." Three different frenzies or madnesses are his gifts to humankind: the warrior in battle, the seer in trance, and the poet in creativity. Subtle, wily, mysterious and dangerous, he often ignores pacts made in honor with humans. Attended by his two ravens, two wolves, and the Valkyries. Feared by ordinary people and worshipped only by princes, poets, the berserkers, and sorcerers. Unpredictable when invoked. Runes, poetry, words of power, sacred poetry, magic, divination, storms, wind, death, rebirth, knowledge, weather, justice, reincarnation, wisdom, the arts, initiation, law, light, music, prophecy, patron of priests, war, inspiration, weapons, horses, deceit, medicine, fate, civilization; patron of poets, sages, and writers.

RAN: "The Ravager"; Vana-Goddess; wife of Aegir. She is unpredictable, and malicious. Drowning, the sea, sailors, storms, great terror.

SIF (siff): Asa-Goddess; Earth Mother; wife of Thorr. She is noted for her beautiful hair. Harvest, fruitfulness, plenty, generosity.

SIGYN (sig-in)/SIGUNA/SIGNY: Goddess wife of Loki; two sons Vali and Narfi. Love, faithfulness, loyalty.

SJOFNA (syof-nah): Goddess of love. One of the Asynjor.

SKADI (skah-dee): "Harm"; daughter of the Giant Thjatsi; wife of Njord. Mountains, winter, hunting, revenge, dark magic.

THORR / THOR / THUNAR / THUNOR/ DONAR; Asa-God; "The Thunderer"; "High Thunderer" champion of the Gods and enemy of the Giants and Trolls; protector of the common man; son of Odhinn and Jord. His symbol is his magic hammer Mjollnir (Destroyer). He has a magic belt (Megingjardar or Strength-Increaser). He drives a chariot pulled by two giant male goats; his wife is Sif. Although he is sometimes over hasty in judgment, he is a totally reliable friend and battle-companion. He has wild red hair and beard; always in battle dress. Strength, law and order, defense, oaks, goats, thunder, lightning, storms, weather, crops, trading voyages, water, courage, trust, revenge, protection, war, battle.

TYR (tier)/TIU/TIWAZ/TIW/ZIU: Asa-God; "The One-Handed"; patron of the Thing or Assembly; called the bravest of the gods. Giver of victory in battle against odds; he is never deceitful. He presides over law, legal contracts, assemblies of the people for judicial matters, awarded victory in combat. The sky, war, athletics, victory in battle, justice, meaningful self-sacrifice, order, bravery, honor, integrity, law and the binding of solemn oaths, courage.

ULL (ool)/ULLR: "The Magnificent"; "the Bow God"; sometimes known as the Death God; son of Orvandel-Egil by the beautiful Sith. God of archery, skiing, winter sports; powerful enchanter. Thrown out of Asgard by Odhinn because the Allfather was jealous. Beauty, hunting, sports, nobility, magic, single combats or contests.

VALKYRIES (val-kye-reez)/WAELCYRIE/ VALKYRJA/IDICI: "Choosers of the Slain"; female warrior-attendants of Odhinn, they direct the course of battles, choosing the valiant warriors for Valhalla. In Old English they were called waelceasig. Tradition says there are thirteen of them. Brynhild as Sigrdrifa (Victory-Giver) was a valkyrie. She initiated Sigurd into runic wisdom. They are helmeted goddesses with spears crowned with flames and mounted on flying horses whose manes drop dew or hail. They can also turn themselves into swan-maidens. They are death angels, mare-women. Associated with horses and wolves. Fearlessness, war, death.

VANIR (vah-near): Fertility Gods of Asgard; second race of deities. Magic powers, witchcraft, also called Vana-Gods.

WELAND / WAYLAND /WIELAND / VOLUND / VOLUNDR: North Germanic god of smiths; Wonder Smith; prince of the fairies; supreme craftsman. A Shape-shifter associated with horses. Mentioned in the tales of Siegfried (Sigurd) and Dietrich of Bern. Strength, cunning, skill, healing, horses, magic, metal-working.

YMIR (im-meer): First Frost Giant. Brutal, evil, violent.

10. Spellwork

The use of certain gestures and words, when performed in a specific way with candles, herbs or other magical equipment, is known as spellwork or spelling.

Spellwork was and is an important part of all pagan religions. Pagans believe in actively participating in the unfoldment of opportunity and development in their lives. They believe that it is their right to confidently petition their deities for what they want. Furthermore, they believe it is their responsibility to do whatever they personally can to aid in gaining their desires. To do this, all pagans engage in some form of spellworking.

Spellwork is a type of magic, the drawing down of energy from another plane of existence. This energy is woven into a specific physical form or result by the use of certain words, gestures, thoughts and practices.

Doing spellwork that will bring results is like exercising a physical muscle of the body. Repetition and practice strengthen the ability to do spelling that will bring about a desired manifestation. Playing at spellwork may bring you what you want a few times, but it is not reliable. Practice and dedication are necessary if you want to have a continued, consistent influence on your own life and the opportunities that come to you.

Before beginning any spellwork, it is a good idea to consecrate your magical weapons, jewelry, wand and other equipment. Rituals of consecration for the wand, sword, dagger and jewelry are listed among the spells of Elf and Dwarf Magic. All other metal tools may be consecrated with the sword ritual, changing the name of the tool in the chant. All other non-metal ritual tools may be consecrated with the wand ritual. This is done within a drawn circle of power.

Wind chimes can be considered as bells. Hung outside, the chimes draw Freyr's attention and blessings when they ring.

Turn to the Tables of Correspondence to check for appropriate deities, colors, incenses, etc. for any spelling. Always choose matching incenses for all your spellwork.

Remember, all spelling to decrease is done during the waning Moon or on the New Moon. All spelling to increase is done during the waxing Moon or on the Full Moon.

Herb Magic

ALDER (*Alnus glutinosa*). This tree yields three dyes: red from the bark, brown from the twigs, and green from the flowers. It is said that the Elves use the green dye from alder.

APPLE OR CRAB APPLE (*Pyrus malus*). Also known as Fruit of the Gods, Fruit of the Underworld, Silver Bough, Tree of Love. An apple cut crosswise will reveal a five-point star, symbol of Freyja and Idhunn. Apples are a Norse symbol of long life. Apple wood can be carved into charms for long life and wisdom. Wands of this wood are used in love rituals. Cider is an excellent substitute for blood when called for in old spells.

ASH, MOUNTAIN (*Fraxinus excelsior* or *F. americana*). An ash twig hung over the doors repels evil, as does scattering the leaves to the four directions around your house. Burning ash wood at Yule (Winter Solstice) brings prosperity. Ash wands are for healing.

AVENS (*Geum urbanum*). Also known as Herb Bennet, Star of the Earth, Yellow Avens, Blessed Herb, Golden Star. Its three leaves represent Thorr, Odhinn and Freyr. An exorcism plant when added to incenses, but when carried it attracts the opposite sex.

BEECH (*Fagus sylvatica*). Ancient runic tablets were often made of this wood as it represents wisdom and creativity. Oracle messages can be heard by listening to the wind through the leaves.

BIRCH (*Betula alba*). Also known as White Birch, Canoe Birch, Paper Birch, Lady of the Woods. Gently striking an outdoor ritual area with a birch twig or branch will drive off all negativity. It was also known as the tree of conception and birth to the Norse.

BISTORT (*Polygonum bistorta*). Also known as Patience Dock, Snakeweed, Dragonwort, Red

Legs. An herb of psychic powers, it can be added to incenses used during divinations. Sprinkle a little in your purse or wallet to draw money.

BLACKTHORN (*Prunus spinosa*). Also known as Sloe, Mother of the Wood. Blackthorn wands are all-purpose and can drive out ghosts and negative spirits. The wood makes good walking sticks because of its protective qualities.

BRACKEN (*Pteridium aquilinum*). A piece of root under your pillow can bring dreams that help with problems.

BRAMBLE (*Rubus fructicosus* or *R. villosus*). Also known as Blackberry, Dewberry, Thimbleberry. Its five leaves, and other five-leafed plants, represent the goddesses, especially Freyja. Its leaves can be used in spells for protection or wealth.

BRIAR (*Rosa rubiginosa* or *R. canina*). Also known as Wild Rose, Briar Rose, Dog Rose. Its petals can be used in incenses for love.

BUTTERCUP (*Ranunculus bulbosus*). Also known as Crowfoot, King's Cup, Pilewort, Goldcup. The flowers can be floated in the cauldron while doing scrying.

CELANDINE (*Chelidonium majus, C. minus, Ranunculus ficaria*). Also known as Tetterwort, Garden Celandine, Swallow Herb, Devil's Milk. Carry it to court to help the judge and jury decide in your favor.

CENTAURY (*Erythraea centaurium*). Also known as Century, Bitter Herb, Feverwort. It is said that snakes will not go where it is planted. Added to incenses it repels negative spirits.

CHAMOMILE (*Anthemis noblis* or *Matricaria chamomilla*). Also known as Roman Chamomile, Dog Fennel, Ground Apple. Roman chamomile is the best, smelling like fresh apples when cut or picked. Added to incenses, it draws prosperity, calmness. Grown around the house or in the garden it reverses spells cast against you.

CLUB MOSS (*Lycopodium clavotum*). Also known as Wolf Claw, Staghorn, Foxtail. A favorite of the gods, this plant and its spores give great blessings and protection.

DANDELION (*Taraxacum officinale*). Also known as Cankerwort, Wild Endive, Lion's Tooth, Blow Ball. If the ripe down blows off without a wind, it will soon rain. To send a message to another person or to the Gods, concentrate while holding a ripe flower. When you have been able to hold the message for about a minute, blow off the flower-down.

ELDER (*Sambucus canadensis*). Also known as Devil's Eye, Lady Elder, Hollunder, Ellhorn, Old Lady, Elderberry. Especially sacred to the German goddess Holda/Bertha. The tree bleeds red sap when cut and absolutely must be asked for permission before cutting. Otherwise it is apt to bring bad luck. Elder wands can be used to exorcise negative spirits from houses or places. To remove warts, rub them with a green twig, then bury it.

ELM (*Ulmus campestris*). Also known as

Slippery Elm, Rock Elm, English Elm, Winged Elm. Its leaves can be sprinkled around a ritual area for protection.

FERNS (all species). Planted near the door it gives protection. When burned outside, it causes rain.

FEVERFEW (*Chrysanthemum parthenium* or *Pyrethrum parthenium*). Also known as Featherfoil, Flirtwort, Pyrethrum. Carry it to prevent sickness and accident.

FIR, SILVER (*Abies alba*). Also known as Birth Tree. To bless and protect a mother and new baby, a flaming fir candle was carried three times around the bed in northern Europe.

HAWTHORN (*Crataegus oxyacantha*). Also known as May Bush, Tree of Chastity, White Thorn, Haw, May Tree. An infusion containing hawthorn blossoms purifies wherever it is sprinkled. Hawthorn wands have great power and are sacred to the Mother Goddesses. Because of its fertility powers, it was used as a decoration at weddings.

ICELAND MOSS. Can be added to prosperity bags or poppits when doing spellwork for increase of money.

IVY (*Hedera spp.*). POISONOUS if eaten. It was carried by brides for good luck and love. A plant of Freyr, it was used as decoration at Yule.

JUNIPER (*Juniperus communis*). Also known as *Gemeiner Wachholder* (common juniper), Gin Berry. It was a holy tree in northern

Europe where it was used with wild thyme in divination and trance incenses.

LILY OF THE VALLEY (*Convallaria magalis*). POISONOUS if eaten. Also known as May Lily, May Bells. It was believed that it sprang from dragon blood. The oil or distilled water from the flowers is said to strengthen the memory when applied to the third eye in the center of your forehead.

LOOSESTRIFE, PURPLE (*Lythrum salicaria*). Also known as Willow-herb, Rainbow Weed. Burned in incenses or sprinkled about the house, it dissolves arguments.

MAIDENHAIR (*Adiantum pedatim*). A fern, this plant brings love and harmony when grown in the house.

MALE FERN (*Dryopteris felix-mas*). The uncurled dried fronds are known as Lucky Hands and bring luck, wealth and love when carried.

MANDRAKE (*Mandragor officinarum, Atropa mandragora*). POISON. Also known as Mandragora, Brain Thief, Gallows, Mannikin, Raccoon Berry, Herb of Circe. Very rare and usually replaced by the American May Apple or the English White Bryony, both of which are POISONOUS. The whole root is placed on the altar for protection if under spell-attack by another. The root can be carved into a tiny human figure and used in image magic.

MARIGOLD (*Calendula officinalis*). Also known as Calendula, Holigold, Marybud, Bride of the Sun, Ruddes. Picked on a Full Moon and used in incenses or washes, it helps one to see Elves and Dwarves. A flower carried in the pocket helps to win favor in court.

MARJORAM (*Origanum majorana*). Also known as Joy of the Mountains, Wintersweet, Sweet Marjoram, Pot Marjoram, Mountain Mint. Used in spell-bags, it relieves depression, brings money and happiness. Use in an infusion with peppermint to cleanse magical tools if undesirable people have handled them.

MISTLETOE (*Viscum album*). POISONOUS if eaten. Also known as Golden Bough, Donnerbesen, Thunderbesom, Birdlime. Sacred to Thorr and Balder, and known in Old Norse as *mistillteinn*. It is an all-purpose herb, capable of protection, granting love and health, bringing money and happiness wherever it is hung.

MUGWORT (*Artemisia vulgaris*). Also known as Naughty Man, Artemisia, Witch Herb, Sailor's Tobacco. A Moon herb, its odor in incenses helps with scrying, divination and clairvoyance.

MULLEIN (*Verbascum thapsus*). Also known as Hag's Taper, Feltwort, Candlewick Plant, Velvet Plant, Velvetback, Shepherd's Club. Oil from its flowers is excellent for children's earaches. Powdered mullein leaves are a good substitute for graveyard dust in old spells. Carry it for courage and to keep away wild animals.

NUTS & CONES. All nuts and cones are sacred to the fertility deities. Double nuts, such as walnuts, are very lucky.

OAK (*Quercus robur, Q. alba*). Also known

as Tanner's Bark, White Oak, Duir. Especially sacred to Thorr because oaks are frequently struck by lightning. Acorns are carried for youthfulness, long life and freedom from illnesses and pain. Plant an acorn on the New Moon to acquire money quickly. Oak wood makes excellent all-purpose wands of great power.

OAKMOSS (*Evernia pruastri*). This grows as a lichen on the oak trees and is a wonderful fixative for scents in incenses. It is also a good additive to gain money and protection.

PEPPERMINT (*Mentha piperita*). Also known as Brandy Mint, Lammint. Drink peppermint tea to help clear head colds, warm the body and increase energy. An infusion sprinkled around the ritual area expels all negativity.

ST. JOHNSWORT (*Hypericum perforatum*). Also known as Goat Weed, Herba John. When picked on Summer Solstice and hung near a window, it drives off lightning and ghosts. Burned, it banishes unwanted spirits.

SALT. Although not an herb, salt is a sacred substance, used by nearly every religious culture in the world. A few grains sprinkled throughout the house will cleanse all vibrations that are negative. This must be repeated every Full Moon.

TANSY (*Tanacetum vulgare*). Also known as Buttons. This plant repels ants and flies. Its lemony fragrance makes a good vibration purifier.

THISTLE, BLESSED (*Carbenia benedicta, Cnicus benedictus, Carduus benedictus*). Also known as Holy Thistle. It can be used in incenses or bouquets to break hexes.

THYME, GARDEN (*Thymus vulgaris*), WILD THYME (*T. serpyllum*). Also known as Common Thyme, Mother of Thyme. One of the Norse sacred herbs burned to purify temples and objects. It is a favorite plant of Elves. Crush a leaf against your third eye in the center of your forehead to enhance your psychic powers.

VALERIAN (*Valeriana officinalis*). Also known as Garden Heliotrope, Vandal Root, Cat's Valerian, Amatilla. This plant has a strong pungent odor that is repelling to some people. But cats are said to love pillows made with this herb. The powdered root is sometimes used in place of graveyard dust called for in old spellworkings. Hung in the home or carried in bags, it protects.

VERVAIN/VERBENA (*Verbana officinalis*; Blue Vervain; *V. hastata*). Also known as Juno's Tears, Enchanter's Plant, Holy Herb, Van-Van, Herb of Enchantment. A Norse sacred herb used in spells of love, cleansing, purification, protection. An infusion sprinkled around the ritual area is good for exorcism and purification. Thriving plants grown in the house or garden provide a steady inflow of money.

WHITE WILLOW (*Salix alba*). Also known as European Willow, Tree of Enchantment, Witches' Aspirin, Withy. It is a Moon tree sacred to all Moon Goddesses and Great Mother Goddesses. Wands made from willow branches are specifically for Moon magic. But willows have been known to cause trouble for anyone cutting their limbs without asking first and leaving a gift.

Tap on a willow with your knuckles to avert evil and accidents.

WOODRUFF (*Asperula odorata*). Also known as Master of the Woods, Woodrove, Wuderove. It acquires its fragrant scent only as it dries. When you wish to change the outlook of your life, carry a few leaves with you. A quarter ounce steeped for nine days in a bottle of wine makes a fine magical and spellworking drink.

WORMWOOD (*Artemisia absinthium*). It is not advisable to eat or drink anything made with this herb as it is addictive and DANGEROUS. Also known as Crown for a King, Absinthe. A very magical herb sacred to the Moon, this herb can be used in incenses for scrying, prophecy, divinations, and astral projection.

YARROW (*Achillea millefolium*). Also known as Seven Years' Love, Sanguinary, Military Herb, Soldier's Woundwort. Its stalks can be used in divination spells and to consult the I Ching. Yarrow tea is drunk to improve your psychic powers.

YELLOW DOCK (*Rumex crispus*). Also known as Curled Dock, Sour Dock. The seeds and powder are used in money spells and incenses.

YEW (*Taxus baccata*). Also known as Chinwood, English Yew, European Yew. POISONOUS. It can be used as decorations at Winter Solstice to symbolize death and endings. It is safer to use the oil rather than the poisonous plant.

Cauldron Magic

Cauldrons come in all sizes, with or without legs. If you use the kind without legs and plan to burn anything very hot in it, place a heat mat underneath to prevent scorching the altar top.

Anytime you use water or other liquids in your cauldron, carefully dry it afterwards to avoid rusting. The same applies whenever you get water on the sword and dagger.

Prophecy: Fill the cauldron half-full of fresh water. Float a few buttercup or marigold petals in it. Light your incense. Be certain that any candles you use do not reflect in the cauldron or shine in your eyes.

Stir the cauldron gently three times with your dagger while chanting softly:

Into the threads of time I cast my
thoughts
To catch a glimpse of what will be.
O Gods of Asgard, bring into my mind
The lovely gift of prophecy.

Lay aside the dagger and look deep into the cauldron. The prophecies may come in immediate visions, strong impressions, or later dreams. This is best done on the Full Moon.

Prophecy: Fill the cauldron half-full of fresh water. Stir the cauldron gently three times with your fingers. With a lighted candle, slowly drip spots of wax into the swirling water. The prophecy is read by interpreting the images seen in the wax, much like reading tea leaves. Boats, clouds and horses usually signify journeys or movement. The Sun, Moon and stars indicate spiritual growth and/or life's successes. Develop your own interpretations for the images. This is best done on the Full Moon.

Healing: Have on the offering plate these herbs: mountain ash leaves or berries, feverfew, vervain. On a small piece of parchment, draw a figure to represent the sick person. This need not be artistic. A stick figure with the person's name underneath will do. Tap the cauldron with your wand, say:

> *Cauldron of the Great Mother,*
> *Cauldron of rebirth and renewal,*
> *Hear my call.*
> *Heal _____ (person's name) of all illnesses.*
> *Rebuild his/her body, mind and spirit.*

Tap the parchment three times with the wand. Light the parchment from one of the altar candles and drop it into the cauldron to burn:

> *All illness turn to ashes,*
> *All wrongness now is right.*
> *My words have reached to Asgard.*
> *Your healing comes tonight.*

Slowly sprinkle the herbs over the ashes. When cool, bury the herbs and ashes in the ground to destroy the illness. This is best done during the waning Moon.

Prosperity: Place the cauldron in the center

of the altar with the offering bowl of milk and
honey by the side. Also have ready a small green
cloth bag. Into the cauldron sprinkle a little
woodruff (for changes in your life), bistort,
chamomile, Iceland moss and vervain. Stir lightly
with your wand while chanting:

> *Come, you Elves and Dwarves of old.*
> *Fill my pockets up with gold.*
> *Small ones, dressed in fur and silk,*
> *I've brought you gifts of honey and milk.*
> *A thank you gift for aiding me*
> *To find luck and prosperity.*

Gather the herbs and stuff them into the bag;
fasten shut by tying or sewing. Hold the bag over
the incense smoke:

> *Blessings to all who come to my aid.*
> *Between friends is this bargain made.*

Carry the bag with you or keep on your altar.
Place the offering bowl outside overnight. Pour
what remains onto the ground in the morning.
This is best done during the waxing Moon.

Love: Set up the altar two days before the
Full Moon with a pink candle in its holder inside
the cauldron, a rose in a vase beside it. Also have
available rose or apple blossom oil and a small bell.
At the same time on each of the two days before the
Full Moon, hold the pink candle and pour loving
thoughts into it. Do not light it until the Full Moon
night. On Full Moon night, carve into the candle
with your dagger the runic equivalent of a "true
love for me." Rub the candle with oil from the wick
down to the end, thus bringing to you the love you

desire.

Set the candle in its holder inside the cauldron and light it. Ring the bell three times. Chant:

As this candle flame grows bright
And ever grows much higher,
Freyr, Lord of Love, please bring to me
Love's ever-burning fire.
Then as the flame does flicker low
Finally to depart,
Freyr, Lord of Love, please give to me
A true love, heart to heart.

Ring the bell three more times. Leave the altar as it is until the candle has burned completely out.

Banishing: Set the cauldron in the center of the altar with the offering plate of salt beside it or on top. Lay the horn to the left of the cauldron. Hold your sword straight out and over the cauldron while you chant:

By the power of oak and ash and thorn, I
  give warning to all negative entities.
Whether you be born of thought or deed, re-
  turn to those who sent you! Begone, foul
  troublemakers! By the power of oak and
  ash and thorn, I say Begone!
If you stay, the Asa-Gods will send you to
  the flames of Muspell and the freezing
  darkness of Hel!
Slink back to your makers! Take up lodg-
  ing in their homes and hearts where you
  belong!
By the power of oak and ash and thorn, and

all the Gods of Asgard, I say DEPART!

Lay the sword on the floor before the altar. Give one long blast on the horn, or shout: "Get out NOW!" Take up the plate of salt and hold it high. Then go through every room and closet of your home, sprinkling a few grains of salt in each corner. Also sprinkle window ledges and door sills. If you feel your car needs cleansing, sprinkle salt in it also, including the trunk space. This is best done during the waning Moon.

Protection: Best done during the waxing Moon. Put your cauldron in the center of the altar with a goblet of wine on the right side, the horn on the left. Inside the cauldron lay a piece of jewelry you will wear to increase the protection. Sprinkle equal parts of chamomile, elder flowers, blessed thistle and vervain on the altar around the cauldron. Then put a little salt over the herbs. Blow the horn three times. Take up your sword and hold it out over the cauldron. Chant 3, 5, 7 or 9 times:

> *Mighty Thorr, your presence is required.*
> *I await your aid and protection.*

Rest your sword point-down on the floor at your feet, holding both hands on the hilt.

> *Champion of the Gods and human-kind, Thorr of the mighty hammer,*
> *Grant me your protection. Defend me against all evil.*
> *Be my champion, great Thorr, in my hour of need.*

Lay the sword on the floor before the altar. Lift up the goblet of wine:

> *For my champion, I offer drink.*
> *And to bond our friendship, I share this*
>   *with You.*

For each drink you take, solemnly hold up the goblet. Save part of the wine to be poured outside as Thorr's share:

> *We have drunk together as comrades. I*
>   *now ask one more boon, mighty*
>   *Thorr.*
> *Bless this jewelry that I may know that*
>   *your hand of protection is with me at*
>   *all times. I do thank you.*

Put on the jewelry. Put out the candles. Gather up the herbs and salt and sprinkle outside.

Binding: This is best done during the waning Moon. Set the cauldron on the altar with a candle holder inside. On a small piece of parchment paper, write the name of the person who is bothering you, or "all my enemies." Anoint the paper with vervain or binding oil and place under the candle holder.

With the dagger, carve four small X's lengthwise on a black candle. As you carve each one, say:

> *One for the Allfather, strong in his hall,*
> *One for Thorr, champion of all,*
> *One for Heimdall, great horn in his*
>   *hand,*
> *One for Freyja, Queen of the land.*

Tie four black threads, one at a time, tightly

around the candle while saying:

> *One to seek them / him / her,*
> *One to find them / him / her,*
> *One to bring them / him / her,*
> *One to bind them / him / her,*
> *Stone to stone, forever one.*
> *So say I. This spell is done.*

Oil the candle from the end to the wick, then roll in a mixture of vervain, valerian and blessed thistle. Place in the holder and light. Allow the candle to burn out completely. Then burn the parchment on the offering plate. Bury or throw away the remaining herbs, parchment ashes and candle wax.

Sword and Dagger Magic

It is Norse tradition to name your sword and dagger. Carefully carve or paint the weapon's name and your magical name in runes on the hilt. See the section in this chapter on Dwarf Magic for consecration rituals for sword and dagger.

To Gain a Desire: Sword and dagger magic is the easiest to do. To gain a desire, go to a secluded area where there is a small patch of bare earth. With your weapon, lightly carve your desire into the ground, then surround it with a circle. When finished, lay your hands on the Earth and whisper:

> *Erce, Erce, Erce, Mother Earth,*
> *Hear my plea.*
> *Send this desire or better to me.*

Walk away without looking back.

Protection of Home and Belongings:
Stand before each window and door with dagger or
sword in hand. Using the weapon, draw the symbol of Thorr's hammer in the air before the open-
ing. This symbol looks like an upside-down capital
T. Go through the house clockwise as when you
draw a circle. As you draw this symbol at the open-
ings, say:

> *By the power of Mjollnir and Thorr,*
> *Nothing and no one wishing me harm*
>   *shall pass this way.*

Increase Visions During Meditation:
Choose a comfortable chair and lay the sword
crosswise about three feet in front of it. Stand beyond the sword, dagger in hand. Beginning on the
right side, and going up and to the left, "cut" a
doorway in the air, then say:

> *Across Bifrost bridge I go to commune*
>   *with the Gods of Asgard.*
> *I will sit beside the Well of Urd for in-*
>   *struction by the Norns.*
> *Freely I go. Freely I return.*

Walk through the door to your chair and begin your meditation. When your meditation is finished, step back across the sword and seal the
doorway with the dagger. This is done by drawing
the doorway from left to right.

Cord Magic

Always choose a color according to your needs
and desires of each particular spellwork. For binding or reversing, do at the waning or New Moon.

For all increase spells, do at the waxing or Full Moon. If you wish the spell to work a very long time, such as with binding spells, use thread instead of cord. Then bury the thread, throw it into a river or out the car window along a busy highway. For other spells, store the cord in a safe secret place. The knots can be untied when the spellwork manifests, and the cord used again at another time.

Hold the cord or thread in both hands and concentrate on what you want done. Begin at one end of the cord and work towards the other end in tying knots. As you tie each knot, chant:

> *By knot of one, this spell's begun.*
> *By knot of two, it will come true.*
> *By knot of three, my power shall be.*
> *By knot of four, this power I store.*
> *By knot of five, this spell's alive.*
> *By knot of six, events I'll fix.*
> *By knot of seven, to Asgard's Heaven*
> *I send my spell for the Gods to see,*
> *To give me aid and enlighten me.*
> *This spell goes out on wings of power*
> *To return full-grown in another hour.*

Elf Magic

See the Tables of Correspondence for colors, herbs, etc. that entice Elves. Be sure to use your quartz and moonstone.

Consecration of the Wand: Best done on the Full Moon. To be put on the altar: offering bowl with milk and honey, offering plate with marigold petals and thyme, crystal and moonstone. Lay the wand in the center of the altar. Light a good blessing incense with a pinch of ginger added. Chant:

> *Light to Light, the call goes out,*
> *To cross the air of space and time.*
> *The power returns from Alfheim,*
> *Drawing Elves sublime.*
> *This wand was made for magic.*
> *Your blessings now need I.*
> *This I ask from friend to friend,*
> *By Earth and plant and sky.*

Gently stroke the wand from the tip towards you, alternately using the crystal and moonstone. Do this for several minutes. If you have named the wand, put that name and your magical name on it in runes, either by carving or painting. Leave the wand on the altar overnight with the offering bowl and plate. Next morning pour the herbs and milk outside.

Plant Magic: If you have a plant that needs special help, or if you are planting a garden, very lightly sprinkle ginger around the plant or edges of the garden to entice the Elves. Place your offering bowl with a little milk and honey by the plant or in the garden on the New and Full Moon. If the plant is indoors, set your crystal quartz or moonstone near it.

Animal Magic: An Elf blessing for pets or wild animals is a good way to establish friendly contact with the Elves. Place an offering of milk and honey with a little ginger sprinkled in it either on your altar or outside in a sheltered place. If possible, lay a few fern fronds by the bowl. Also lay out your crystal and moonstone. With your wand, gently tap the bowl three times and say:

> *Light Elves, listen. Hear my call.*
> *Your presence here I ask.*
> *For _____(animal's name) needs your*
>   *protection.*
> *To safeguard him/her is your task.*
> *Keep _____(animal's name) safe by*
>   *night and day,*
> *While asleep or while at play.*
> *Beautiful Light Elves, answer me.*
> *I ask your presence here.*
> *To this little one protection give*
> *That he/she may have no fear.*
> *Blessings to all who come to my aid.*
> *Between friends is this bargain made.*

This spell may also be used to protect children. Light Elves and children have a strong affinity for each other.

Herb Blessing: Best done during the waxing Moon or on the Full Moon. Any herbs you plan to use for Norse magic should be blessed as soon as possible. Put them in their containers, and set all the containers on your altar. Burn a good blessing incense to which you have added a pinch of ginger. Have marigold petals and thyme on the offering plate on the altar also. Stand before the altar with wand in hand:

> *Light Elves, come now. Join with me*

To bless these herbs most merrily.

Rest the wand briefly on each container. Then tap the offering plate:

As you have given to me, so I give to you.

Leave the offering plate on the altar overnight. Then sprinkle the herbs outside.

House and Property Blessing: Best done on the Full Moon. Have on the altar: two small blue or green cloth bags, offering plate with thyme and ginger, two small pieces of parchment with the words *Light Elves* written in runes on them, crystal and moonstone. Burn a blessing incense. Tap the bags, parchments, and plate with your wand:

Light Elves, come, both Lord and Lady,
From your home in forests shady.
Give your blessings now to me,
And we shall be friends happily.

Fold the parchment into small squares, and put one in each bag. Sprinkle a small amount of herbs into each bag. Save some of the herbs to put outside for the Elves. Leave the bags between the crystal and moonstone on the altar overnight. You can then hang one in your house and one in your car. Change the herbs and repeat the chant each Full Moon.

Dwarf Magic

See the Tables of Correspondence for the correct incense, herbs, colors, etc. Be sure to use your pyrite and steel or iron.

Consecration of Sword and Dagger:
Best done between the New and Full Moons. Burn
a good blessing incense with a pinch of cinnamon
added. Lay your sword and dagger on the altar between the pyrite and steel or iron. Chant:

> *From the mountains good Dwarves bold*
> *Often came in times of old,*
> *With their magic and their spells.*
> *Now I ask you come to me.*
> *Spell-bind this sword and dagger here.*
> *That magic filled these weapons be.*
> *Good Dwarves, magical and bold,*
> *Join with me as in times old.*

Gently stroke both the sword and dagger
from tip to hilt with the pyrite and metal. Do this
for several minutes. Call each weapon by the
name you have chosen for it before replacing it on
the altar. If you have not carved or painted its
name in runes on the hilt, along with your magical
name, do so now. Leave them on the altar overnight.

Blessing Magical Jewelry: Burn a blessing incense with a pinch of cinnamon added. Lay
your magical jewelry inside the cauldron on the altar between the pyrite and metal. Raise your dagger over the cauldron and chant:

> *Hammers, hammers, underground,*
> *Hammers sounding in the dark.*
> *Good Dwarves, listen unto me.*
> *Good Dwarves, harken. Hark!*
> *Make this jewelry magical,*
> *Gleam of silver and of gold,*

> *Master Smiths, bring help to me,*
> *That magic power I may hold.*

Put each piece of jewelry on the tip of the dagger blade, and pass it slowly through the incense smoke. Leave on the altar overnight.

Stone Magic: Anytime you purchase anything containing a gemstone, or are working with stones in any manner, such as landscaping, gardens, etc., ask the Good Dwarves for blessings, aid and protection. Be sure to leave them sprinklings of cinnamon, thyme and marigold petals. Use this chant:

> *Stones, stones, bones of Mother Earth,*
> *Dwelling place and delight of all Good*
> *   Dwarves,*
> *Harken to the words of the Master*
> *   Smiths and Miners,*
> *Who speak chants of protection and aid.*
> *Bend your Earth-powers to help me.*
> *Circle your deep power to protect me.*
> *Master Smiths and Miners, walk in*
> *   peace.*

House and Property Blessing: This may be combined with the blessing by the Light Elves. Burn a good blessing incense. Have on the altar: your dagger, pieces of pyrite and steel or iron, two small dark green or brown cloth bags, two small pieces of parchment with the words *Good Dwarves* written on them in runes, offering plate with cinnamon and thyme. Tap the bags, parchments and plate lightly with your dagger. Chant:

Good Dwarves, in your caverns deep,
Hear my words. Watch with me keep.
Give your blessings now to me,
And we shall be friends happily.

Fold the parchment into small squares and put one in each bag. Sprinkle small amounts of herbs into each bag. Save some herbs to put outside for the Dwarves. Leave the bags between the pyrite and metal overnight. You can then hang one in your house and the other in your car. Change the herbs and repeat the chant each Full Moon. This can be done in conjunction with the similar spell for Light Elves.

Rune Magic

Nordic-Germanic runes were a magical alphabet, later used to write ordinary messages. Because they were usually carved in wood or stone, there were few curved lines. There were some variations from country to country, but basically they were similar enough to be read by any knowledgeable rune-master or magician.

The carved runes were painted red to embody them with magical power. In ancient Germanic the words for "to make red" and "to endow with magical power" were the same.

In Old Norse, the word *run* meant secret lore, wisdom and magical signs. In Old English, *run* meant mystery and secret, the same as it did in Old Saxon. The word in Old High German was *runa*, meaning mystery, secret or to whisper a secret.

Rune-masters were identified by their deep blue cloaks and the leather charm pouches at their belts. Often they carried a staff carved with runes and capped with a bronze mounting. Rune-masters, whether male or female, were treated with great honor and respect.

Some runic alphabets had more letters than others. There were also powerful symbols frequently found in Nordic rock carvings but not considered part of the Elder Runes; among these were Thorr's hammer, the ship, the World Tree, the wealth symbol, two types of the Sun-wheel, and the Moon.

This chapter contains a table which lists the 24 Elder Runes, the deity or deities connected with them, their magical meanings, and other important features. Following this table is a description of the seven mystical runes. The runes can be used to write out spells or put names on magical objects.

The 24 Elder Runes are traditionally divided into groups of eight runes each. Freyja's Eight are: *fehu, uruz, thurisaz, ansuz, raidho, kaunaz, gebo,* and *wunjo.* Hagal's (World Tree) Eight are: *hagalaz, naudhiz, isa, jera, ehwo, perdhro, elhaz, and sowilo.* Tyr's Eight are: *tiwaz, laguz, berkano, eihwaz, mannaz, ingwaz, othalaz,* and *dagaz.*

To use the runes for divination, paint or etch each rune on one side of a thin one-inch square of wood or a small flat stone. (See the previous chapter on magical tools.)

Before using the runestones in any form of divination, hold the bag in your hands and say:

> *Allfather Odhinn, Rune-Master,*
> *Lead me to true knowledge*
> *Of the sacred runes.*
> *Freyja, Mistress of Magic,*
> *Vana-Goddess of seidr,*
> *Reveal to me the future paths.*

Keep the runestones in a bag large enough to get your hand inside. Gently stir the runestones and say:

> *Urd! Verthandi! Skuld!*

Without looking, draw out three. Lay them out in a horizontal line, starting from the left. The left stone will be the past, the center the present, and the right stone the future. If the future position is unclear, you may draw up to three more runestones to clarify it.

Use the magical meanings from the table to interpret the reading. The negative meanings of each rune apply to the reversed position or if the rune lies next to another rune that must be read in the negative.

Five stones may also be drawn and placed in the Cross of Thorr for reading. This layout is an equal-armed cross: one runestone in the middle, representing the person for which the reading is being done; one above this; one below this; and one on each side of the middle runestone. The middle rune is the person involved. The two runes flanking it are the present conditions affecting the question. The bottom rune is past conditions still having an influence, and the top is the future.

Another way of foretelling by the runes is to cast them on a square piece of cloth or fur. This is done by selecting nine runes without looking. Hold them in your hands and say:

> *Allfather Odhinn, Rune-Master,*
> *Lead me to true knowledge*
> *Of the sacred runes.*
> *Freyja, Mistress of Magic,*
> *Vana-Goddess of seidr,*
> *Reveal to me the future paths.*

Hold the runestones in your hands over the cloth and concentrate on your question. Gently toss the runes away from you onto the cloth while saying:

> *Urd! Verthandi! Skuld!*

The nearest runes are read as the past or things moving away from the questioner. The further out on the cloth the further into the future is the influence. Any runes that land with the rune not showing are not read. This also applies to any runes that do not fall on the cloth.

Elder Rune Table

Rune: ᚠ

Alphabet: F
Norse Name: *Fehu, Feoh, Fe*—Cattle, fee, money,
   gold.
Tree: Elder
Deity: Aesir
Color: Light red
Tarot Card: Tower
Astrology: Aries
Magical Meaning: Money, property, fulfillment,
   good luck, dynamic power, goals reached.
   Negative: A person or offer to be avoided.

Rune: ᚢ

Alphabet: U, V
Norse Name: *Uruz, Ur*—Ox, aurochs, drizzle,
   rain.
Tree: Birch
Deity: Vanir
Color: Dark green
Tarot Card: High Priestess
Astrology: Taurus
Magical Meaning: Advancement, good fortune,
   happiness, basic powers of manifestation. If near
   negative, bad luck, minor illnesses.

Þ

Rune:

Alphabet: TH

Norse Name: *Thurisaz, Thorn, Thurs*—Giant,
   thorn, the good one, the strong one.

Tree: Oak

Deity: Thorr

Color: Bright red

Tarot Card: Emperor

Astrology: Mars

Magical Meaning: Journey over water. Good
   news from a distance. Inner strength to break
   resistance or pass a time of waiting. Take great
   care in making decisions. Negative: Delayed or
   unpleasant journey.

Rune: ᚨ

Alphabet: A

Norse Name: *Ansuz, Oss, Ass*—Asa, god, ances-
   tral god, one of the Aesir.

Tree: Ash

Deity: Odhinn

Color: Dark blue

Tarot Card: Death

Astrology: Mercury

Magical Meaning: Transformation, new goals,
   information that changes your life. Negative:
   Bad advice.

Rune: ᚱ

Alphabet: R

Norse Name: *Raidho, Reidh, Rit, Rad*—Long
   journey on horseback, chariot, riding, wagon.

Tree: Oak
Deity: Forseti
Color: Bright red
Tarot Card: Hierophant
Astrology: Sagittarius
Magical Meaning: Journey, getting to the truth, seeing past illusions. If near negative, travel problems, inconvenience, blocks.

Rune: ⟨

Alphabet: C, K
Norse Name: *Kenaz, Kaon, Cen, Kaun*—Torch, swelling, sore, boil, forge, hearth, pyre.
Tree: Pine
Deities: Freyja; Dwarves; Weland; Loki
Color: Light red
Tarot Card: Chariot
Magical Meaning: The rune of craftsmen and the crafty or sly. Controlled energy for dissolution. Life-strength, ambition, determination, inspiration. Negative: Bad judgment, confusion.

Rune: X

Alphabet: G
Norse Name: *Gebo, Gifu, Gyfu, Gipt*—Blessing, gifts from the Gods, hospitality, generosity.
Trees: Ash, elm
Deities: Odhinn; Freyja
Color: Deep blue
Tarot Card: Lovers
Astrology: Pisces
Magical Meaning: The exchange of force or power

between the gods and humans. Wedding, legacies, promotion, windfall. Negative: Sadness caused by someone close.

Rune: Þ

Alphabet: W

Norse Name: *Wunjo, Wynn, Wunna, Vend*—Bliss, pleasure, joy, delight, hope, pasture.

Tree: Ash

Deities: Freyr; Elves

Color: Yellow

Tarot Card: Strength

Astrology: Leo

Magical Meaning: Security, comfort, happiness, good social life.   Negative: Needless self-sacrifice.

Rune: Н

Alphabet: H

Norse Name: *Hagalaz, Haegl, Hagal*—Hail, snow

Trees: Yew, ash

Deity: Ymir

Color: Light blue

Tarot Card: World

Astrology: Aquarius

Magical Meaning: Ability to bring opposites into harmony. Delays waiting for the right time. Negative: Setbacks, delays, situations out of your control.

Rune:

Alphabet: N
Norse Name: *Naudhiz, Nyd, Naut, Nau-dhr*—Need, necessity, distress.
Tree: Beech
Deities: Norns
Color: Black
Tarot Card: Devil
Astrology: Capricorn
Magical Meaning: Distress that clouds reality, something out of the past that drives you (not necessarily good). Caution needed to succeed. Negative: Impatience leads to disaster.

Rune:

Alphabet: I
Norse Name: *Isa, Iss, Eis*—Ice
Tree: Alder
Deities: Frost (or Rime) Giants
Color: Black
Tarot Card: Hermit
Astrology: Moon
Magical Meaning: Period of absolute stillness. Be careful what you say. Negative: Hasty words bring trouble; indifference, uncaring, detached emotions.

Rune:

Alphabet: J (pronounced *y*)
Norse Name: *Jera, Ger, Yer, Ar, Jer*—Good year,

harvest, good season.

Tree: Oak

Deities: Freyr

Color: Light blue

Tarot Card: Fool

Astrology: Earth

Magical Meaning: A cycle, time, reaping rewards, no quick results.

Rune: ⌐

Alphabet: EI, I, Y

Norse Name: *Eihwaz, Eoh, Yr, Ihwar*—Mountain ash, yew tree

Tree: Yew

Deities: Odinn; Ull

Color: Dark blue

Tarot Card: Hanged Man

Astrology: Scorpio

Magical Meaning: End of a matter, situation or problem. Drastic change. Death of a relationship. Negative: Old conflicts and situations cause trouble.

Rune: ⟨

Alphabet: P

Norse Name: *Perdhro, Perodh, Peorth, Pear*— Fate, dice cup.

Tree: Beech

Deities: Norns

Color: Black

Tarot Card: Wheel of Fortune

Astrology: Saturn

Magical Meaning: Chance, unexpected material gain, surprise. If near negative, a secret that can hurt you.

Rune: ᛉ

Alphabet: Z
Norse Name: *Elhaz, Eolh, Aquizi, Ihwar*—Elk, stone axe, protection, yew bow.
Tree: Yew
Deities: Valkyries
Color: Gold
Tarot Card: Moon
Astrology: Cancer
Magical Meaning: Visible movement, blockages removed. If near negative, people actively trying to stop you.

Rune: ᛋ

Alphabet: S
Norse Name: *Sowilo, Sigil, Sig, Sol*—Sun, Sun-wheel
Tree: Juniper
Diety: Balder
Colors: White, Silver
Tarot Card: Sun
Astrology: Sun
Magical Meaning: Change, guidance, time of renewal, drastic changes, complete turnaround, advancement of plans, change of residence. Negative: Failure which leads to new opportunities.

Rune: ↑

Alphabet: T
Norse Name: *Tiwaz, Tyr, Tiu, Tir*—Sky god, the
   god Tyr.
Tree: Oak
Deities: Tyr; Mani
Color: Bright red
Tarot Card: Justice
Astrology: Libra
Magical Meaning: Unbiased wisdom, justice, law
   and order. Justified victory and success.
   Negative: Intrigue, deception, others working
   against you.

Rune: ᛒ

Alphabet: B
Norse Name: *Berkano, Beorc, Birca*—Birch tree,
   birch goddess.
Tree: Birch
Deities: Frigg; Nerthus; Hel
Color: Dark green
Tarot Card: Empress
Astrology: Virgo
Magical Meaning: Creativity, new beginnings,
   birth, marriage. If near negative rune,
   failure, divorce, miscarriage, stagnant period.

Rune: ᛗ

Alphabet: E
Norse Name: *Ehwo, Eoh, Ehwaz, Eh*—Horse,
   steed, stallion, war horse.

Trees: Oak, ash
Deities: Freyja; Freyr
Color: White
Tarot Card: Lovers
Astrology: Gemini
Magical Meaning: Trust, self-transformation, new attitude, new home, new goals, steady progress. If near negative, progress blocked.

Rune: ᛗ

Alphabet: M
Norse Name: *Mannaz, Man, Madhr*—Mankind, world, human being.
Tree: Holly
Deities: Heimdall; Odhinn
Color: Deep red
Tarot Card: Magician
Astrology: Jupiter
Magical Meaning: Man, lover or husband; male influence in life. New career opportunities. Positive link with the Gods. Negative: Material loss.

Rune: ᛚ

Alphabet: L
Norse Name: *Laguz, Lagu, Lögr*—Lake, water; or *laukaz*—leek
Tree: Willow
Deities: Njord; Balder
Color: Deep green
Tarot Card: Star
Astrology: Moon

Magical Meaning: Hidden movement below the surface, no progress seen but it is happening. Life energy; manifestation coming from other planes. If near negative, behind the scenes action blocks progress, usually with a woman involved.

Rune: ◇

Alphabet: NG
Norse Name: *Ingwaz, Ingvi, Ing*—Kin, the god Ing (later a name for Freyr).
Tree: Apple
Deities: Ing; Freyr
Color: Yellow
Tarot Card: Judgment
Astrology: Moon's quarters
Magical Meaning: Creating life-force at work. Family, relatives, children, parents, spouse. Benefits from relatives. Negative: Family becomes a burden.

Rune: ⋈

Alphabet: D
Norse Name: *Dagaz, Dag, Daeg*—Day
Tree: Spruce
Deity: Odhinn
Color: Light blue
Tarot Card: Temperance
Astrology: Dark of the Moon
Magical Meaning: Sudden realization, awakening, mystic light, attraction between two people.

Rune: ◇

Alphabet: O
Norse Name: *Othalaz, Ethel, Odal, Odhal, Othala*—Homeland, property, inherited land, sacred enclosure
Tree: Hawthorn
Deities: Odhinn; Thorr
Color: Deep yellow
Tarot Card: Moon
Astrology: Full Moon
Magical Meaning: Inborn qualities, tangible possessions. If near negative, illusions, jealousy greed, wasted efforts.

Mystical Runes

Rune: ⟋⟍

Norse Name: A form of the Sun-wheel (triskelion)
Colors: Gold, white
Magical Meaning: Motion, movement, advancement of plans. Possible change of residence. If near a negative, someone or something keeps you from moving ahead.

Rune: 𐰞

Norse Name: Unknown
Colors: Green, gold
Magical Meaning: Wealth, material success,

gain. If near a negative, you must work hard to
gain success.

Rune:

Norse Name: Thorr's hammer
Color: Red
Magical Meaning: Increase, protection, will
power, magical power under control. Overpowers
all negative runes.

Rune:

Norse Name: World Tree
Color: Green
Magical Meaning: Protection through magical
workings. Cosmic guidance in everyday life.
Overpowers all negative runes.

Rune:

Norse Name: Sun-wheel
Colors: Gold, white
Magical Meaning: Inner guidance, protection,
seeking mystical truths. If near a negative, bad
advice, gullibility.

Rune:

Norse Name: Moon
Colors: Silver, white
Magical Meaning: Orderly change, psychic
abilities. Negative: Chaos, false information.

Rune:

Norse Name: Ship
Color: Blue
Magical Meaning: Growth, movement, journeys, transmutation of problems into positive situations. Negative: Stagnation, problems growing more burdensome.

11. *Tables of Correspondence*

Norse Deities

Name: Aegir
Also Called: the Alebrewer
Colors: turquoise, purple
Incense/Oil: rose, cedar
Symbols: dolphin, whale
Stones/Metals: coral, turquoise, lapis lazuli,
           amethyst, tin
Plants: avens, rose, polypody, oak, verbena
Day: Thursday
Runes: *laguz, naudhiz*
Chant: Hail, Alebrewer, Vana-God of the sea,
       Wind and wave obey your command.
       Turn always a smiling face toward me.
       Give only good things from your hand.
       Alebrewer, Wave-Roller, god of the deep,
       Aegir, watery Van, bring me good to keep.

Name: Audhumla
Also Called: Nourisher; Mother Earth

Colors: green, brown
Incense/Oil: juniper, jasmine, lotus
Symbol: cow
Stones/Metals: quartz crystal, smoky topaz,
      copper
Plants: loosestrife, mugwort, rose, willow, birch,
      fir, hawthorn
Day: Monday
Runes: *uruz, hagalaz*
Chant: Mother Earth, Nourisher, great
      mother of old,
        Your nourishment keeps from your
          children the cold.
        Mother Earth, Mother of birth,
        Nourisher, Thought-Flourisher,
        Bless my family and my hands.
        Bless my home and all my lands.
        May my house be bright, my future
          right.

Name: Balder, Baldr, Baldur
Also Called: the Bright One; Shining God; the
    Bleeding God; Sun God
Colors: gold, white
Incense/Oil: frankincense, cinnamon
Symbol: the Sun
Stones/Metals: gold, goldstone
Plants: ash, chamomile, celandine, marigold,
  mistletoe, St. Johnswort
Day: Sunday
Runes: *sowilo, fehu, raidho*
Chant: Bright One, Shining God, Light for all
      to see, Open up my inner eyes.
      Grant me harmony.

Help me bring my life to balance.
Give me wisdom and advice,
To make the next incarnation
A better, happier life.

Name: Bragi
Also Called: Patron of skalds and minstrels; master of eloquence
Colors: orange, multi-colored
Incense/Oil: sandalwood, storax
Symbols: harp, book
Stones/Metals: agate, carnelian, alloys
Plants: fern, lily of the valley, maidenhair, mandrake, marjoram, valerian, beech
Day: Wednesday
Runes: *mannaz, dagaz, gebo, othalaz*
Chant: See the Master Poet.
Hear his glorious song.
Wise is he and eloquent,
Writing sagas long.
Grant me creativity,
The arts as my destiny.
Bless me, Master Poet.
Sing a magic song.

Name: Forseti
Also Called: God of justice
Color: yellow
Incense/Oil: rose, cedar
Symbol: scales
Stones/Metals: lapis lazuli, amethyst, aquamarine, tin
Plants: avens, rose, polypody, oak, verbena
Day: Thursday

Runes: *naudhiz, ehwaz, perdhro, elhaz*
Chant: Justice, peace, tranquility,
   Talents of the god Forseti.
   Stretch out your soothing hand.
   Wipe clean the marked life sand.
   Sweep away the tears and strife.
   Bring calm and justice to my life.

Name: Freyja, Freya
Also Called: Lady; Seer; Great Goddess; the
   Sage; Freyja of the Black Swordhand;
   Queen of the Valkyries
Color: red—physical love
   black—protection, revenge
   silver or green—all other aspects
Incense/Oil: rose, sandalwood, mint, floral scents
Symbols: cat, number 13, boar, the Full Moon,
   horse and sword, necklace, Brising-
   amen, 5-pointed star
Stones/Metals: amber, emerald, jade, malachite,
   moonstone, silver, copper
Plants: alder, birch, bramble, elder, feverfew,
   mint, mugwort, rose, tansy, thyme,
   vervain, yarrow, apple, valerian
Day: Friday
Runes: *kaunaz, fehu, uruz, tiwaz*
Chant 1: (as Seer and Lady)
   Great Goddess, Mistress of cats,
   Lady of love, beautiful Vana-
    Goddess,
   Fulfill my greatest needs, O glorious
    one.
   Teach me the magic I need.
   Give me a glimpse of your deep

wisdom.
Teach me in dreams. Enrich my life.
O Lady, you are Golden-Tears of
   Asgard.
Lady of love, beautiful Vana-
   Goddess,
You are the Shape-shifter, the Sayer,
The Independent One.
Give me the strength and the magic I
   need.

Chant 2: (as Valkyrie leader)
Queen of the warrior-women,
Freyja of the Black Swordhand,
Mistress of Magic, enchantments deep,
You who beckon to fallen heroes,
Harken to this, your child.
I would weave strong magic for protection,
Deep magic to bind and chasten.
I lift up my sword to repel all attackers.
Beware, foul troublemakers!
For Freyja whispers her spells in my ear.
Freyja, Queen of the Valkyries, stands at
   my side.

Name: Freyr, Frey, Fro
Also Called: the Lord; the Lover; Sun God; god of
      Yule
Colors: red—physical aspect
   green or gold—other aspects
Incense/Oil: mint, sandalwood, rose
Symbols: boar, the Sun
Stones/Metals: goldstone, rose quartz, gold, brass,
      bronze

Plants: avens, mountain ash, ivy, holly, nuts and
cones, St. Johnswort, yew.
Day: Friday
Runes: *sowilo, ingwaz, jera, ansuz, raidho*
Chant: The Lord, the Lover,
Vanir god of the Sun and wealth,
Hear me, great Freyr.
Fill my life with good things,
Sun and rain to bless the Earth.
Happiness, peace and love
To satisfy the body.
Abundance, bravery and honor
To feed the soul.
Green groves to worship in,
And other believers in the Old Gods
To fill those groves with joy again.

Name: Frigg, Frigga, Frija
Also Called: Queen of the Gods; Mother Goddess
Colors: silver, blue
Incense/Oil: lily of the valley
Symbol: crown
Stones/Metals: moonstone, quartz, crystal,
silver, copper
Plants: birch, fir, hawthorn
Day: Monday
Runes: *berkano, uruz, dagaz, mannaz*
Chant: Asa-Mother, Queen of Asgard,
Loving wife and mother, yet holder of
infinite wisdom.
Show me the way to reconcile opposites in
my life:
Independence and commitment,
Giving and receiving,

Destiny and changing-magic.
Teach me the cleverness to be all needed
   things,
Yet to remain myself, apart and free.
Aesir Mother, bless me.

Name: Gefion, Gefjun
Also Called: the Giver; Mistress of Magic
Colors: green, gold
Incense/Oil: floral scents
Symbols: plow, wheat, corn
Stones/Metals: amber, malachite, copper
Plants: hawthorn, alder, wheat, corn, elder,
      thyme, yarrow
Day: Friday
Runes: *gebo, fehu, jera*
Chant: Fertility Lady, the Giver,
      Mistress of the growing land,
      Guide my steps in magic
      Till fate turns in my hand.
      Change my luck and fortune;
      Show me what I need
      To grow in art and wisdom.
      Gefion, my magic power feed.

Name: Gullveig, Heid
Also Called: Golden Branch; Gleaming One
Color: gold
Incense/Oil: frankincense, cinnamon, amber
Symbol: the Sun
Stones/Metals: topaz, jacinth, chrysolite, gold,
      copper
Plants: ash, chamomile, celandine, marigold,
      mistletoe, St. Johnswort

Day: Sunday
Runes: *sowilo, eihwaz, dagaz, tiwaz*
Chant: Golden Branch, Gleaming One,
    Guide of seers and prophecy,
    Vanir sorceress, Healer divine,
    Aid and instruct me.

Name: Heimdall
Also Called: the White God; Guardian of Bifrost
Colors: white, multi-colors
Incense/Oil: birch
Symbols: horn, rainbow
Stones/Metals: aquamarine, amethyst, gold,
    copper, bronze
Plants: avens, rose, polypody, oak, verbena
Day: Thursday
Runes: *mannaz, elhaz, eihwaz, tiwaz, ingwaz*
Chant: Guardian of Bifrost bridge,
    Blower of the great horn Gjall,
    Beginnings and endings are influenced by
      your hand.
    Influence my fate.
    End old events of my life smoothly.
    Make new and better beginnings for me.
    Heimdall, White God, hear me!

Name: Hel, Hela
Also Called: Queen of the Dead
Color: black
Incense/Oil: storax, myrrh
Symbols: wolf, dog
Stones/Metals: onyx, jet, obsidian, black agate,
    lead
Plants: beech, elm, elder, yew, ivy, juniper,

mullein, blackthorn, willow

Day: Saturday

Runes: *hagalaz, isa, ehwo*

Chant: Dark mistress of Sleet-Den,
    Queen of the land of ice and snow,
    You whose hands gather evil ones
    To stay in your land below.
    Goddess Hel of Death and Darkness,
    You delight in revengeful clashes.
    Goddess of the Dead and Niflheim,
    Let my enemies taste defeat and ashes.

Name: Hermod

Also Called: the Brave One

Color: red

Incense/Oil: dragon's blood, pepper

Symbols: sword, shield

Stones/Metals: bloodstone, garnet, ruby, red
    topaz, red agate, iron, steel

Plants: thistle, hawthorn, pine, woodruff,
    wormwood

Day: Tuesday

Runes: *tiwaz, ingwaz, eihwaz, elhaz*

Chant: Asa-God, son of the Allfather,
    You who braved the ride into the kingdom of
      Hel
    To ask the return of the Shining God,
    Help me to find honor and bravery,
    The treasured virtues that grant entrance
      into Asgard.

Name: Hoenir, Honir

Also Called: the Silent One

Color: red

Incense/Oil: pine

Symbols: shield, helmet

Stones/Metals: bloodstone, garnet, ruby, red
 topaz, red agate, iron, steel

Plants: thistle, hawthorn, pine, woodruff, wormwood

Day: Tuesday

Runes: *elhaz, eihwaz, othala*

Chant: Asa-God, silent warrior,
 Whose thoughts lie only in bravery and
 warrior-skill,
 Help me to defend myself.
 Teach me to be silent until the time for
 defense comes.

Name: Holda, Holde, Holle, Hulda, Bertha,
 Berchta

Also Called: White Lady; the Crone; Dark Moon
 Goddess; Black Earth Mother

Color: black

Incense/Oil: storax, myrrh

Symbols: wolf, bear

Stones/Metals: onyx, jet, obsidian, black agate,
 lead

Plants: beech, elm, ivy, juniper, mullein,
 blackthorn, willow, yew, elder

Day: Saturday

Runes: *isa, hagalaz, ehwo*

Chant: White Lady of the Wild Hunt,
 Crone Lady of the Moon,
 Change the fate that rules me,
 Lift all curses soon.
 To all who ill-wish me,
 Fire and cold,

Their lives be in ashes,
Crone Lady of old.

Name: Idhunn, Idun
Also Called: Keeper of the Golden Apples
Colors: silver, green
Incense/Oil: apple blossom
Symbol: apples
Stones/Metals: quartz, crystal, smoky topaz,
    copper
Plants: loosestrife, mugwort, rose, willow, birch,
    fir, hawthorn
Day: Monday
Runes: *elhaz, eihwaz, othalaz*
Chant: Asa-Goddess of immortality,
    Keeper of the wondrous golden apples,
    Grant me the youth and long life of the Gods,
    Youth and enduring life of the mind as well
      as of the body.
    Let my keyword be flexibility,
    That my expansion in the realm of magic
    May be unending.

Name: Loki
Also Called: Father of Lies; the Trickster;
    Shape-Changer
Color: black
Incense/Oil: dragon's blood, pepper, yew
Symbol: snake
Stones/Metals: onyx, jet, obsidian, black agate,
    lead
Plants: beech, yew, elm, ivy, juniper, mullein,
    thistle, blackthorn, willow, elder
Day: Saturday

Runes: *thurisaz, naudhiz, kaunaz*
Chant: 1: (as Master Thief)
> A thief has taken what is mine.
> Return it all, Loki divine.

Chant 2: (other aspects)
> Oath-Breaker, Troublemaker,
> Master of Lies,
> Blood-brother of Odhinn,
> From whom truth flies.
> Cunning deceiver, evil spell-weaver,
> Skillful Shape-Changer,
> Son of Giant, Asgard-defiant,
> Keep me from danger.
> Cunning and fire, treacherous liar,
> Come to my aid.
> Teach me your daring, mischievous faring,
> That trouble be made.
> Wondrous dark magic, Loki, teach me,
> But harken that my spirit stays free.

Name: Mimir, Mimr, Mimi
Also Called: the Wise One
Color: yellow
Incense/Oil: cinnamon
Symbols: fountain, pool, well
Stones/Metals: topaz, jacinth, chrysolite, gold, copper
Plants: ash, chamomile, celandine, marigold, mistletoe, St. Johnswort
Day: Sunday
Runes: *mannaz, othala, dagaz, laguz, ehwo, ansuz*
Chant: Asa-God whose great wisdom is kept at the Fountain of Midgard,

Give me water from that Fountain.
Give me calmness, calm as the waters you
    rule,
Peace and knowledge,
Knowledge to deal rightly with all events,
And creativity to make needed changes.

Name: Nanna, Nana, Anna, Inanna
Also Called: the Moon; Great Mother; Earth
    Goddess
Colors: silver, pale green
Incense/Oil: juniper, jasmine, lotus, floral scents
Symbol: crescent Moon
Stones/Metals: moonstone, quartz, silver
Plants: hawthorn, mugwort, rose, willow, birch,
    fir, loosestrife
Day: Monday
Runes: *uruz, berkano, wunjo*
Chant: Gentle Nanna, Great Goddess mild,
    Great Mother, harken to me, your child.
    Grant me, Lady of the Moon,
    Enduring love, and that right soon.

Name: Nehallennia
Also Called: the Fruitful One
Colors: green, yellow
Incense/Oil: rose, sandalwood, floral scents
Symbol: cornucopia
Stones/Metals: amber, emerald, jade, malachite,
    moonstone, silver, copper, bronze
Plants: alder, birch, bramble, elder, feverfew,
    mugwort, rose, tansy, thyme, vervain,
    yarrow
Day: Friday

Runes: *berkano, uruz, wunjo, laguz*
Chant: Horn of plenty in your hand,
     Great Nehallennia, bless this land.
     Fruitfulness, plenty, ripening seed.
     Abundant Goddess, this I do need.

Name: Nerthus, Erce
Also Called: Earth Mother
Colors: green, light brown
Incense/Oil: juniper, jasmine, lotus
Symbols: groves, the sea
Stones/Metals: quartz, crystal, smoky topaz,
    copper
Plants: loosestrife, mugwort, mint, rose, willow,
    birch, fir, hawthorn
Day: Monday
Runes: *berkano, ehwo, wunjo, laguz, dagaz,
    raidho*
Chant: Erce, Erce, Erce, Nerthus,
    Wise Earth Mother, Goddess of groves,
    Purify me. Bless me.
    Prepare me for great growth and blessings.

Name: Njord
Also Called: Sea-Ruler
Color: blue
Incense/Oil: vervain, cedar
Symbols: the sea, ships, fish
Stones/Metals: aquamarine, amethyst, turquoise,
    tin
Plants: avens, polypody, all ferns, oak, oak moss,
    verbena
Day: Thursday
Runes: *laguz, fehu, mannaz, othala, eihwaz*

Chant: Wise Njord, Vana-God of the sea,
    Prosper, protect, give wisdom to me.
    Father of the Lady and Lord,
    Let us be of one accord.

Name: Odhinn, Odin, Wodan, Woden, Othinn
Also Called: Allfather; Great Father; All-Seeing;
    Frenzied; God of the Wild Hunt
Colors: black—revengeful and dark aspects
    red—weather, justice, healing
    orange—other aspects
Incense/Oil: pine, dragon's blood, sandalwood
Symbols: raven, wolf, eagle
Stones/Metals: onyx, jet, agate, carnelian, alloys,
    tin, gold
Plants: polypody, all ferns, maidenhair,
    mandrake, marjoram, valerian, beech, yew
Days: Wednesday, Saturday
Runes: *wunjo, jera, ansuz, dagaz, othala, laguz,
    ingwaz, ehwo*
Chant: 1: (as Allfather, Rune-Master)
    Patron of those who write and sing,
    Rune-Master, whose craft was learned
    By self-sacrifice and dedication,
    Show me the words of power.
    Lead me on the paths of creativity.
    Stand by me at initiation into realms of
        magic.
    Let me call upon your wisdom and magic.
    All-Seeing, Great Father, hear my call.

Chant 2: (as Lord of the Wild Hunt)
    Blue cloak swirling in the storm,
    Hat pulled low over empty eye.

Ravens at your shoulders, wolves by your
  feet,
Lord of the Wild Hunt who rides Sleipnir
Across the stormy skies,
With warrior-women armed for battle.
Protect me from my enemies.
You who grasp my fate in your fist,
Turn that fate into paths of success.

Name: Ran
Also Called: the Ravager
Color: black
Incense/Oil: juniper, storax, dragon's blood
Symbols: stormy sea, nets
Stones/Metals: onyx, jet, obsidian, black agate,
  lead
Plants: beech, elm, yew, ivy, juniper, mullein,
  blackthorn, willow, elder
Day: Saturday
Runes: *thurisaz, naudhiz, kaunaz*
Chant: Vana-Ravager, malicious sea-woman,
  Calm the storm. Grant me safe journeys.
  Hold back the terrors of the mind.
  Let my life be on still waters.

Name: Sif, Siff
Also Called: Earth Mother; Golden Hair
Colors: gold, green
Incense/Oil: jasmine, all floral scents
Symbols: loom, mirror
Stones/Metals: quartz, crystal, smoky topaz,
  copper, bronze, brass
Plants: mugwort, chamomile, rose, willow, birch,
  fir, hawthorn

Day: Monday
Runes: *wunjo, berkano, gebo, jera*
Chant: Beautiful Sif, you of the long golden hair,
  Good-hearted Earth Mother of Aesir,
  Help me to harvest the plans I have sown.
  Let my life show forth fruitfulness and
    plenty.

Name: Sigyn, Siguna, Signy
Also Called: the Faithful
Colors: pink, brown
Incense/Oil: all floral scents
Symbol: bowl
Stones/Metals: quartz, crystal, smoky topaz,
    copper, bronze
Plants: mugwort, rose, willow, birch, fir, hawthorn
Day: Monday
Runes: *sowilo, wunjo, uruz*
Chant: Loyal Sigyn, wife devoted,
  Intercede with wayward Loki.
  Show him love and tenderness
  To put his mischievous heart at rest.
  Loyal Sigyn, wife devoted,
  Calm the troublesome Trickster Loki.

Name: Sjofna
Also Called: no other names
Color: red
Incense/Oil: rose, sandalwood, mint
Symbol: heart
Stones/Metals: amber, emerald, malachite, jade,
    moonstone, silver, copper
Plants: alder, birch, elder, mugwort, rose, thyme,
    vervain, yarrow

Day: Friday
Runes: *wunjo, gebo*
Chant: Mysterious Sjofna, Goddess of love,
    Whose tale there is no telling.
    Bring a lover unto me
    That will set my heart to swelling
    With fulfillment and desire.
    Let us be as one.
    Mysterious Sjofna, Goddess of love,
    Let this wish be done.

Name: Skadi
Also Called: no other names
Color: black
Incense/Oil: dragon's blood, pepper, myrrh
Symbols: mountains, New Moon
Stones/Metals: onyx, jet, obsidian, black agate, tin
Plants: blackthorn, beech, elm, yew, ivy, juniper,
    mullein, willow, elder
Day: Saturday
Runes: *thurisaz, isa, kaunaz, hagalaz, ehwo*
Chant: Mistress of dark magic,
    Lady of mountains and winter snow,
    Chase my enemies far away,
    To Hel's dark realm make them go.

Name: Thorr, Thor, Thunar, Thunor, Donar
Also Called: the Thunderer; High Thunderer
Color: red
Incense/Oil: pine, juniper, dragon's blood
Symbols: double-headed axe, goats, lightning
Stones/Metals: carnelian, red agate, lodestone,
    steel, iron
Plants: thistle, avens, oak, oak moss, acorns

Day: Thursday
Runes: *thurisaz, eihwaz, ingwaz, raidho, ansuz*
Chant: 1: (as Defender)
> High Thunderer, Champion,
> Wielder of mighty Mjollnir,
> Ride your great chariot to my defense.
> Preserve me against my enemies.
> Let my life be filled with rightness.
> Let there be order and strength.
> Great Thorr of the red hair,
> Come to my aid.

Chant 2: (as Weather God)
> Mjollnir flies from your mighty hand.
> Storm clouds gather o'er the land.
> Release the warm and nourishing rain.
> Let the Earth be green again.

Name: Tyr, Tiu, Tiwaz, Tiw, Ziu
Also Called: the One-Handed
Colors: yellow, orange
Incense/Oil: pine, juniper
Symbols: sword, helmet
Stones/Metals: smoky topaz, grey agate, steel, bronze
Plants: thistle, oak, juniper, blackthorn, vervain
Day: Tuesday
Runes: *tiwaz, jera, kaunaz, thurisaz, ingwaz, eihwaz*
Chant: Asa-God of the one hand,
> Bravest of all the Gods,
> Hear my plea for justice.
> Stand beside me in the courts,
> Or any time I am accused.

Speak into the ears of those in authority.
Grant me freedom from all persecution.

Name: Ull, Ullr
Also Called: the Magnificent
Colors: white, yellow
Incense/Oil: sandalwood, pine
Symbols: bow, skis, mountains
Stones/Metals: agate, carnelian, alloys
Plants: fern, maidenhair, mandrake, marjoram,
     valerian, beech
Day: Wednesday
Runes: *ehwo, isa, perdhro, tiwaz*
Chant: Powerful enchanter, Magnificent One,
     Let the victory be mine.
     Abilities and beauty, magic skillful,
     Aid me in my endeavors.

Name: Weland, Wayland, Wieland, Volund,
     Volundr
Also Called: Wonder Smith; Prince of the Fairies
Color: yellow
Incense/Oil: juniper, vervain, thyme
Symbols: anvil and hammer, horseshoes
Stones/Metals: agate, carnelian, jasper, steel,
     iron, bronze
Plants: all ferns, marjoram, valerian, thyme,
     beech, juniper
Day: Wednesday
Runes: *elhaz, perdhro, tiwaz, eihwaz, ingwaz*
Chant: See the Wonder Smith at his forge.
     Hear his hammer ring.
     Metal is changed by his strong hands
     Into a beauteous thing.

Magic healer of cunning and skill,
Friend of Dwarf and Elf,
Good luck and strength, power of your hands,
These things I ask for myself.

Name: Light Elves
Also Called: the Little People or Hidden People
Colors: silver, green, blue
Incense/Oil: ginger, lily of the valley, fir, floral
    scents, milk and honey
Symbols: leaf, vine, star, bow and arrow, horses,
    wand
Stones/Metals: silver, quartz, rock crystal,
    moonstone, copper, bronze
Plants: alder, marigold, thyme, all ferns, fir, pine
Chant: Light Elves, from dark forests shady,
    Come to me, both Lord and Lady.
    Dressed in magic clothes and flowers,
    Teach me in the twilight hours.
    Sing to me an eldritch tune
    As the clouds flow past the Moon.
    Whisper magic of the land,
    Mushroom ring and wooded strand.
    Light Elves, from the forests shady,
    Come to me, both Lord and Lady.

Name: Good Dwarves
Also Called: the Master Smiths
Colors: yellow, gold, brown, dark green
Incense/Oil: ginger, cinnamon, spicy scents, milk
    and honey
Symbols: anvil and hammer, all jewelry and
    weapons, swords
Stones/Metals: gold, pyrite, steel, iron, goldstone,

diamond, zircon
Plants: marigold, all ferns, fir, juniper, pine
Chant: Hammers ring in caverns deep,
    Where you, Dwarves, your watch do keep.
    Teach me magic of Earth and stone,
    Gems and metals, Earth Mother's bone.
    From deep mountain caves of yore,
    Come to teach me ancient lore.
    Friend I'll be and secrets keep
    If you teach me magic deep.
    Dwarves of knowledge strong and old,
    Come as once you did of old.

Quick Reference

ABUNDANCE: Nerthus, Freyr, Njord, Freyja, Nehallennia, Dwarves.

ADVICE: Balder, Freyja, Sif, Tyr.

AGRICULTURE: Odhinn, Freyr, Gefion, Sif, Thorr, Light Elves.

AIR: See Sky.

ANIMALS: Frigg, Freyja, Odhinn, Freyr, Loki, Thorr, Light Elves.

ARTS & CRAFTS: Holda, Bragi, Mimir, Odhinn, Weland, Freyja, Sif, Ull, Light Elves, Dwarves.

BEAUTY: Freyja, Sif, Balder, Freyr, Idhunn, Loki, Ull, Light Elves.

BEGINNINGS: Heimdall, Tyr.

BLACKSMITHS: See Metalworking.

BLESSINGS: Balder, Freyja, Heimdall, Njord, Odhinn, Sif, Light Elves, Dwarves.

BOATS: Njord, Aegir, Freyr, Nehallennia, Ran, Thorr.

BRAVERY: See Courage.

BREWING: Aegir.

CALM: Balder, Hodur, Mimir.

CHANGE: Freyja, Loki, Odhinn, Tyr, Njord, Light Elves, Dwarves.

CHARMS: See Magic.

CHILDBIRTH: Frigg, Freyja, Audhumla.

CHILDREN: Audhumla, Frigg, Sif, Sigyn, Light Elves.

CIVILIZATION: Odhinn, Tyr.

COMMERCE: Nehallennia, Freyja, Freyr, Thorr.

COMPASSION: See Mercy.

CONTRACTS: Tyr, Freyr, Njord, Thorr.

COURAGE: Thorr, Tyr, Odhinn, Valkyries, Freyr, Freyja, Hermod, Hoenir, Loki.

CREATIVITY: Freyja, Bragi, Odhinn, Weland, Light Elves, Dwarves.

CREATOR GOD/GODDESS: Freyja, Nerthus, Audhumla, Odhinn.

CRYSTAL READING: See Psychic Abilities.

CUNNING: Loki, Odhinn, Bragi, Frigg, Thorr, Weland, Dwarves.

CURSING: See Revenge.

DARKNESS: Hel, Skadi, Odhinn, Holda.

DEATH: Hel, Ran, Tyr, Valkyries, Freyja, Loki, Odhinn.

DECEPTION: Loki, Odhinn, Thorr, Freyja.

DESTINY: See Fate.

DESTRUCTION: Hel, Loki, Thorr, Odhinn, Ran.

DISASTER: Loki, Ran, Odhinn.

DISEASE: Hel.

DIVINATION: See Psychic Abilities.

DOMESTIC ARTS: Audhumla, Sif, Sigyn, Frigg.

DREAMS: Freyja, Odhinn.

EARTH GOD/GODDESS: Freyr, Nanna, Nerthus, Audhumla, Sif.

EARTHQUAKES: Loki.

ECSTASY: See Passion.

ELOQUENCE: Bragi, Forseti, Odhinn, Tyr, Light Elves.

ENCHANTMENTS: See Psychic Abilities.

ENDINGS: Heimdall, Tyr.

ENLIGHTENMENT: See Blessings.

EVIL: Loki, Aegir, Ran.

FAMILY: See Marriage, Motherhood.

FATE: Holda, Odhinn, the Norns, Freyja, Valkyries, Frigg, Gefion, Tyr.

FERTILITY: Freyja, Frigg, Nerthus, Freyr, Gefion, Nehallennia, Sif.

FIRE: Loki, Freyja, Weland.

FISHING: Nehallennia, Njord. See Boats.

FLOWERS: Freyja, Light Elves.

FORESTS: See Woodlands.

FREEDOM: Odhinn, Thorr, Freyja, Tyr.

GENTLENESS: Balder, Nanna, Sigyn, Sif.

GREAT FATHER: The male principle of creation; god of winter, the Sun, woodlands, forests, animals, the sky, sexual love. Odhinn.

GREAT GOD/GODDESS: Nanna, Freyja, Frigg, Odhinn.

GREAT MOTHER: The female principle of creation; goddess of fertility, the Moon, summer, flowers, love, healing, the seas, water. Nanna.

GROVES: See Woodlands.

GROWTH: Freyr, Nerthus, Nehallennia.

HAPPINESS: Freyja, Freyr, Balder, Sif, Sigyn.

HARMONY: Balder, Sif, Sigyn.

HARVESTS: Balder, Thorr, Sif, Odhinn, Gefion,
Freyr. See Agriculture.

HEALING: Gullveig, Odhinn, Weland, Light
Elves.

HERBS: Freyja, Gefion, Sif, Light Elves.

HORSES: Freyr, Odhinn, Valkyries, Freyja,
Weland.

THE HUNTER: Odhinn.

HUNTING: Skadi, Odhinn, Thorr, Ull.

THE HUNTRESS: Holda, Skadi.

ILLNESS: See Disease, Healing.

ILLUSION: See Shape-Shifter.

INDEPENDENCE: Frigg, Thorr, Freyja, Odhinn, Tyr.

INITIATION: Odhinn, Freyja, Skadi, Thorr.

INSPIRATION: Odhinn, Freyja, Light Elves,

Dwarves.

INTELLIGENCE: See Wisdom.

INVENTIONS: Odhinn, Weland, Light Elves, Dwarves.

JEWELRY: Freyja, Weland, Odhinn, Light Elves, Dwarves.

JOURNEYS: Njord, Thorr, Odhinn, Loki, Freyja, Nerthus.

JUDGMENT: Tyr, Odhinn, Forseti, Thorr.

JUSTICE: Forseti, Thorr, Tyr, Odhinn.

KARMA: See Fate, Retribution.

LAW: Odhinn, Tyr, Forseti, Thorr.

LEARNING: See Wisdom, Arts.

LIFE: Odhinn, Balder, Idhunn.

LIGHTNING: Thorr.

LONG LIFE: Idhunn, Freyja, Odhinn.

LOVE: Freyja, Frigg, Freyr, Nanna, Sigyn, Sjofna.

LUCK: Freyja, Gefion, Odhinn, Thorr, Freyr, Light Elves, Dwarves.

MAGIC: Freyja, Frigg, Odhinn, Freyr, Ull, Gefion, Gullveig, Thorr, Weland, Light Elves, Dwarves.

MAGIC, DARK: Skadi, Holda, Hel, Freyja, Loki, Odhinn. See Spells.

MARRIAGE: Frigg, Sigyn, Sif.

MEDICINE: Gullveig, Odhinn, Light Elves. See Healing.

MERCY: Freyja, Balder, Nerthus, Nehallennia.

METALWORKING: Weland, Mimir, Dwarves.

MISCHIEF: Loki, Odhinn.

MOON: Frigg, Holda, Freyja, Nanna.

MOTHER GODDESS: Frigg, Audhumla.

MOTHERHOOD: Freyja, Frigg, Audhumla.

MOUNTAINS: Skadi, Dwarves.

MUSIC: Odhinn, Bragi, Freyja, Light Elves.

NATURE: See Woodlands.

NIGHT: Hel, Holda, Loki, Odhinn.

OATHS: See Contracts.

OPPORTUNITIES: Odhinn, Thorr, Tyr, Freyja.

ORDER: Tyr, Forseti, Thorr.

PASSION: Frigg, Freyja, Freyr.

PATRON OF PRIESTS: Odhinn, Freyr.

PATRONESS OF PRIESTESSES: Freyja, Skadi.

PEACE: Nerthus, Freyr, Forseti, Mimir, Tyr.

PLEASURE: See Passion.

POETRY: See Writing.

POLITICS: Forseti.

POWER: Odhinn, Thorr, Tyr, Weland, Freyja, Holda, Skadi.

PROBLEM-SOLVING: Odhinn, Forseti, Thorr, Tyr, Freyja, Weland.

PROPHECY: See Psychic Abilities.

PROSPERITY: Nehallennia, Nerthus, Njord, Aegir, Freyja, Freyr, Gefion, Odhinn, Sif, Thorr, Light Elves, Dwarves.

PROTECTION: Thorr, Freyr, Freyja, Heimdall, Odhinn, Tyr, Light Elves, Dwarves.

PSYCHIC ABILITIES: Freyja, Frigg, Gullveig, Odhinn, Skadi, Light Elves, Dwarves, Holda, Loki, Ull. See Blessings, Magic, Spiritual Illumination.

PURIFICATION: Freyja, Frigg, Odhinn, Freyr, Nerthus, Light Elves.

RAIN: Freyr, Thorr, Odhinn.

RAINBOW: Heimdall.

RECONCILIATION: Balder. See Peace.

REINCARNATION: Odhinn, the Norns, Balder.

REMOVE DIFFICULTIES: Balder, Odhinn, Thorr, Tyr, Light Elves, Dwarves, Weland.

RENEWING: See Growth.

RESPONSIBILITY: Idhunn, Hermod, Thorr, Tyr, Forseti.

RETRIBUTION: Odhinn, Tyr, Thorr, Holda, Loki. See Revenge.

REVENGE: Thorr, Holda, Hel, Loki, Odhinn, Ran, Skadi, Freyja, Weland.

RITUALS: Freyja, Odhinn, Light Elves.

RUNES: See Psychic Abilities.

SEA: Nehallennia, Ran, Njord, Aegir, Thorr, Freyja, Freyr, Nerthus.

SEXUAL LOVE: Freyja, Freyr, Frigg, Loki, Sjofna.

SHAPE-SHIFTER: Loki, Odhinn, Freyja, Frigg, Gefion, Light Elves, Dwarves.

SKY: Freyja, Odhinn, Thorr, Tyr.

SNAKE: Loki.

SORCERESS/SORCERER: Loki, Freyja, Gullveig, Odhinn, Ull.

SPELLS: Loki, Freyja, Odhinn, Light Elves, Dwarves. See Psychic Abilities, Magic.

SPIRITUAL ILLUMINATION: Odhinn, Freyja, Light Elves.

SPORTS: Ull, Tyr.

SPRINGTIME: Nerthus.

STORMS: Thorr, Odhinn, Holda, Loki, Ran.

STRENGTH: See Power.

SUCCESS: Nehallennia, Nerthus, Tyr, Balder, Njord, Odhinn, Thorr, Light Elves, Dwarves.

SUN: Balder, Freyr, Odhinn.

TEACHING: Mimir, Odhinn, Freyja, Light Elves, Weland.

THIEVES: Loki.

THUNDER: Thorr.

TRANCE: See Psychic Abilities.

TREASURE: Aegir, Dwarves.

TRICKERY: Loki, Odhinn, Thorr.

TRIPLE GOD: Freyr, Thorr, Odhinn.

TRIPLE GODDESS: Idhunn, Freyja, Hel (or Holda, Skadi)

TRUTH: Odhinn, Forseti, Freyja, Light Elves.

THE UNDERWORLD: Hel.

VICTORY: Odhinn, Thorr, Tyr, Freyja, Ull, Skadi.

VOLCANOES: Loki.

WAR: Valkyries, Tyr, Thorr, Odhinn, Freyja, Hoenir, Loki.

WARNING: Heimdall, Odhinn, Thorr, Tyr.

WATER, FRESH: Mimir, Nerthus.

WEAPONS: Thorr, Valkyries, Freyr, Hoenir, Odhinn, Tyr, Dwarves.

WEATHER: Odhinn, Thorr, Aegir, Freyr.

WHIRLPOOLS: Ran.

WIND: Aegir, Thorr, Odhinn.

WINTER: Holda, Skadi, Freyr, Hodur, Odhinn, Ull.

WISDOM: Frigg, Odhinn, Balder, Bragi, Freyja, Mimir, Njord, Tyr, Light Elves, Dwarves.

WITCHCRAFT: Holda, Freyja, Nerthus.

WOODLANDS: Freyr, Nerthus, Skadi, Thorr, Light Elves.

WRITING: Bragi, Odhinn, Freyja, Mimir.

YOUTH: Idhunn, Balder.

BIBLIOGRAPHY

Guirand, Felix, Editor. *Larousse Encyclopedia of Mythology.* London: Hamlyn Pub., 1978.

Beyerl, Paul. *Master Book of Herbalism.* Custer, WA: Phoenix, 1984.

Blum, Ralph. *The Book of Runes.* New York: St. Martins, 1982.

Branston, Brian. *Gods and Heroes From Viking Mythology.* New York: Schocken Books, 1982.

Budge, E. A. Wallis. *Amulets and Superstitions.* New York: Dover, 1978.

Burton, Richard. *The Book of the Sword.* New York: Dover, 1987.

Campbell, Joseph. *Hero With a Thousand Faces.* Princeton, NJ: Princeton University Press, 1973.

Campbell, Joseph. *The Masks of God.* 3 Vols. New York: Penguin, 1977.

Carylon, Richard. *Guide to the Gods.* Wm. Morrow and Co., date unknown.

Chubb, Thomas Caldecot. *The Northmen.* Cleveland, OH: World Pub. Co., 1964.

Cavendish, Richard. *Mythology: An Illustrated Encyclopedia.* New York: Rizzoli International Pub., 1980.

Cotterell, Arthur. *A Dictionary of World Mythology.* New York: Perigree, 1979.

Davidson, H. R. Ellis. *Gods and Myths of the Viking Age.* New York: Bell Publishers, 1964.

D'Aviella, Count G. *Migration of Symbols.* Wellingborough, UK: Aquarian, 1979.

Eichler, Lillian. *The Customs of Mankind*. Garden City, NY: Nelson Doubleday, 1926.

Evans, Cheryl and Anne Millard. *Norse Myths and Legends*. Tulsa, OK: EDC Publishing, 1986.

Froncek, Thomas. *The Northmen*. New York: Time-Life Books, 1974.

Gayley, Charles. *Classic Myths*. New York: Ginn and Co., 1939.

Gibson, Michael. *The Vikings*. East Sussex, UK: Wayland, 1972.

Hall, Manley Palmer. *Secret Teachings of All Ages*. Los Angeles, CA: Philosophical Society, 1977.

Herzberg, Max J. *Myths and Their Meaning*. New York: Allyn & Bacon, 1928.

Howard, Michael. *The Magic of the Runes*. New York: Samuel Weiser, 1980.

Howard, Michael. *The Runes and Other Magical Alphabets*. Wellingborough, UK: Aquarian, 1981.

Huson, Paul. *Mastering Herbalism*. New York: Stein and Day, 1983.

Klindt-Jensen, Ole and Svenolov Ehren. *The Viking World*. New York: Robert B. Luce, 1967.

LaFay, Howard. *The Vikings*. Washington, DC: National Geographic, 1972.

Lindow, John. *Myths and Legends of the Vikings*. Santa Barbara, CA: Bellerophon Books, 1979.

Line, David and Julia. *Fortune-Telling by Runes*. Wellingborough, UK: Aquarian, 1984.

Lippman, Deborah. *How to Make Amulets,*

Charms, and Talismans. New York: M. Evans and Co., 1974.

Magnusson, Magnus. *Viking Hammer of the North*. London: Orbis, 1976.

McKenzie, Donald. *German Myths and Legends*. New York: Avenel, 1985.

Miller, Richard. *The Magical and Ritual Use of Herbs*. New York: Destiny Books, 1983.

Newark, Timothy. *The Barbarians*. Dorset, UK: Blandford, 1985.

Owen, Gale. *Rites and Religion of the Anglo-Saxons*. New York: Dorset, 1985.

Palsson, Hermann and Paul Edwards. Translators. *Seven Viking Romances*. New York: Penguin Books, 1985.

Rackham, Arthur. *Wagner's "Ring"*. New York: Dover, 1979.

Savage, Anne. *Anglo-Saxon Chronicles*. England: Dorset, 1983.

Serraillier, Ian. *Beowulf the Warrior*. New York: Scholastic Books, 1970.

Simpson, Jacqueline. *Everyday Life in the Viking Age*. New York: Dorset, 1967.

Sturluson, Snorri. *King Harald's Saga*. New York: Dorset, 1986.

Thomas, William and Kate Pavitt. *The Book of Talismans, Amulets and Zodiacal Gems*. No. Hollywood, CA: Wilshire Book Co., 1970.

Thorsson, Edred. *Futhark*. York Beach, ME: Samuel Weiser, 1984.

Thorsson, Edred. *Runelore*. York Beach, ME: Samuel Weiser, 1987.

Walker, Barbara. *Women's Encyclopedia of Myths and Secrets*. New York: Harper and Row,

1983.

Wise, Terence. *Saxon, Viking and Norman Arms*. London: Osprey Publishers, 1979.

Yarwood, Doreen. *Encyclopedia of World Costume*. New York: Bonanza, 1986.

ORDER LLEWELLYN BOOKS TODAY!

Llewellyn publishes hundreds of books on your favorite subjects! To get these exciting books, including the ones on the following pages, check your local bookstore or order them directly from Llewellyn.

Order Online:
Visit our website at www.llewellyn.com, select your books, and order them on our secure server.

Order by Phone:
- Call toll-free within the U.S. at 1-877-NEW-WRLD (1-877-639-9753). Call toll-free within Canada at 1-866-NEW-WRLD (1-866-639-9753)
- We accept VISA, MasterCard, and American Express

Order by Mail:
Send the full price of your order (MN residents add 7% sales tax) in U.S. funds, plus postage & handling to:

> **Llewellyn Worldwide**
> **P.O. Box 64383, Dept. 0-87542-137-7**
> **St. Paul, MN 55164-0383, U.S.A.**

Postage & Handling:
Standard (U.S., Mexico, & Canada). If your order is:
Up to $25.00, add $3.50
$25.01 - $48.99, add $4.00
$49.00 and over, FREE STANDARD SHIPPING
(Continental U.S. orders ship UPS. AK, HI, PR, & P.O. Boxes ship USPS 1st class. Mex. & Can. ship PMB.)

International Orders:
Surface Mail: For orders of $20.00 or less, add $5 plus $1 per item ordered. For orders of $20.01 and over, add $6 plus $1 per item ordered.

Air Mail:
Books: Postage & Handling is equal to the total retail price of all books in the order.
Non-book items: Add $5 for each item.

Orders are processed within 2 business days. Please allow for normal shipping time. Postage and handling rates subject to change.

CELTIC MAGIC
D. J. Conway

Many people, not all of Irish descent, have a great interest in the ancient Celts and the Celtic pantheon, and *Celtic Magic* is the map they need for exploring this ancient and fascinating magical culture.

Celtic Magic is for the reader who is either a beginner or intermediate in the field of magic. It provides an extensive "how-to" of practical spell-working. There are many books on the market dealing with the Celts and their beliefs, but none guide the reader to a practical application of magical knowledge for use in everyday life. There is also an in-depth discussion of Celtic deities and the Celtic way of life and worship, so that an intermediate practitioner can expand upon the spellwork to build a series of magical rituals. Presented in an easy-to-understand format, *Celtic Magic* is for anyone searching for new spells that can be worked immediately, without elaborate or rare materials, and with minimal time and preparation.

0-87542-136-9, 240 pp., mass market, illus.   **$5.99**

THE RITES OF ODIN
Ed Fitch

The ancient Northern Europeans knew a rough magic drawn from the grandeur of vast mountains and deep forests, of rolling oceans and thundering storms. Their rites and beliefs sustained the Vikings, accompanying them to the New World and to the Steppes of Central Asia. Now, for the first time, this magic system is brought compellingly into the present by author Ed Fitch.

This is a complete source volume on Odinism. It stresses the ancient values as well as the magic and myth of this way of life. The author researched his material in Scandinavia and Germany, and drew from anthropological and historical sources in Eastern and Central Europe.

A full cycle of ritual is provided, with rites of passage, magical spells, divination techniques, and three sets of seasonal rituals: solitary, group and family. *The Rites of Odin* also contains extensive "how-to" sections on planning and conducting Odinist ceremonies, including preparation of ceremonial implements and the setting up of ritual areas. Each section is designed to stand alone for easier reading and for quick reference. A bibliography is provided for those who wish to pursue the historical and anthropological roots of Odinism further.

0–87542–224–1, 360 pp., 6 x 9, illus., softcover $17.95

NORTHERN MYSTERIES & MAGICK
Runes & Feminine Powers
Freya Aswynn

The runes are more than an ancient alphabet. They comprise a powerful system of divination and a path to the subconscious forces operating in your life. *Northern Mysteries & Magick* emphasizes the feminine mysteries and the function of the Northern priestesses. It unveils a complete and personal system of the rune magick that will fascinate students of mythology, spirituality, psychism, and Teutonic history, for this is not only a religious autobiography but also a historical account of the ancient Northern European culture.

Discover how the feminine Mysteries of the North are represented in the runes, and how each of the major deities of Northern Europe still live in the collective consciousness of people of Northern European descent. Chapters on runic divination and magick introduce the use of runes in counseling and healing.

1-56718-047-7, 288 pp., 6 x 9, bookmark   **$14.95**